Clean
Car Wars

How Honda and Toyota
are Winning the Battle of
the Eco-Friendly Autos

Clean Car Wars

How Honda and Toyota
are Winning the Battle of
the Eco-Friendly Autos

Yozo Hasegawa

Translated by Tony Kimm

WILEY

John Wiley & Sons (Asia) Pte. Ltd.

Other Wiley Editorial Offices

John Wiley & Sons, Inc., 111 River Street, Hoboken, NJ 07030, USA
John Wiley & Sons, Ltd., The Atrium, Southern Gate, Chichester,
    West Sussex P019 8SQ, UK
John Wiley & Sons (Canada), Ltd., 5353 Dundas Street West, Suite 400, Toronto,
    Ontario M9B 6H8, Canada
John Wiley & Sons Australia Ltd., 42 McDougall Street, Milton, Queensland 4064,
    Australia
Wiley-VCH, Boschstrasse 12, D-69469 Weinheim, Germany

Library of Congress Cataloging-in-Publication Data

ISBN   978-0-470-82329-3

Typeset in 10.5/13 point, Garamond by C&M Digitals (P) Ltd.
Printed in Singapore by Saik Wah Press Pte. Ltd.
10 9 8 7 6 5 4 3 2

Contents

Preface

January 7, 2007. As I stood in the hall of the Cobo Center in downtown Detroit, Michigan, for the opening of the North American International Auto Show (Detroit Auto Show), I felt warm. The last time I was in this city, near the Canadian border, it was buried under a blanket of snow. If global warming was advancing as rapidly as reported, then perhaps it had reached the Motor City just in time to loom over the centennial celebration of the auto industry's premier event.

But early 2007 is also likely to be remembered for something other than the show's centenary. For the first time in as long as practically anyone can remember, General Motors Corp. (GM) would be unseated as the largest auto company in the world—by Toyota Motor Corp. While it seemed that GM would regain the crown by the end of the fiscal year, the event seemed to symbolize that a new automotive age was upon us, one marked by different rules and conditions.

Most of the buzz generated on the floor of the auto show centered on the battle over the next generation of green technologies. This was an aspect of the show that had never really commanded center stage until Toyota's successful launch in 1997 of the Prius, the first mass-produced hybrid passenger vehicle in the world. Powered by a combination of gasoline engine and electric motor, the Prius got 50 percent higher fuel efficiency than most standard gasoline cars, produced significantly lower tailpipe emissions, and sold like hot cakes. If steadily rising oil prices and global warming were not sufficient factors for inducing automakers to start churning out greener cars, then this certainly was.

Both GM and Ford Motor Co. unveiled their latest plug-in hybrid electric vehicles (PHEVs), recently touted by U.S. President George W. Bush as a solution to an automotive future not dependent on oil. DaimlerChrysler AG (now just Daimler AG) announced a next-generation, clean-burning, diesel automobile designed to reduce smog and acid-rain producing nitrogen oxide (NO_x) emissions significantly.

Japanese automakers Toyota and Honda Motor Co. were looking to take advantage of the early lead they had achieved with their hybrid technology. Both companies were increasingly being perceived as eco-conscious compared with their American competitors, and winning over U.S. consumers as a result.

Given the milieu of maddening prices at the pump and mounting environmental concerns, both of which have become market-driving forces, I came away from the show reinforced in my belief that strong clean-car strategies and the technology they generate will, sooner than later, become the key determining factors of success and survival in the automotive world.

Toyota hurried to build on the success of the Prius by rolling out hybrid iterations throughout its lineup, including its luxury brand, the Lexus. Metrically, Toyota would seek to become the world's largest auto company in sales at nine million vehicles in 2007, with the goal of breaching the ten million mark in 2008. But in a January 5 New Year's gathering for Japan's three powerful economic business associations—the Japan Business Federation (*Nippon Keidanren*), the Japan Chamber of Commerce and Industry, and the Japan Association of Corporate Executives (*Keizai Doyukai*)— Toyota president Katsuaki Watanabe chose to downplay quantitative goals, emphasing basic execution and improvements in quality.

"Toyota must not only focus its technological development on the environment, safety, and energy, but remain an exemplary manufacturing company in terms of quality, cost, and human resources development."

Honda was coming off a strong year in 2006, in which it overtook Nissan Motor Co., Ltd. to become Japan's number two automaker. Honda hopes to once again demonstrate to the world that it has what it takes to lead the green-technology charge under its research-centric president, Takeo Fukui, with development of its own sophisticated hybrid and diesel technologies, along with near-term commercialization of a groundbreaking fuel-cell vehicle.

Both Honda and Toyota would look to their roots for clues to success in the twenty-first century. In Chapter 1, I describe how the Toyota Prius evolved from a vaguely stated managerial directive aimed at "redefining the passenger car for a new age," the vision of company founder, Kiichiro Toyoda.

U.S. automakers, by contrast, continued to be plagued by problems: slumping sales and the burdens of restructuring, compounded by the need to invest heavily in the new technologies that are reshaping the automotive landscape. But they're not to be counted out, and are certainly capable of coming back strongly.

GM CEO Rick Wagoner, upon learning his company had been overtaken by Toyota in first-quarter sales, pledged to "fight for every sale." Both GM and Ford unveiled promising environmental initiatives of their own at the 2007 Detroit Auto Show. Dieter Zetsche, president of then DaimlerChrysler, chose to stress his company's interest in productivity and profits over sales volume, while focusing on its leadership in greener diesel technologies, an area in which European automakers are making great strides.

In his Academy award-winning documentary, *An Inconvenient Truth*, former U.S. Vice President Al Gore shows a slide that depicts Toyota and Honda surging ahead of U.S. automakers in sales volume. "If you look at who's doing well in the world, it's the companies that are building more efficient cars," Gore points out. The film goes on to urge viewers to buy a hybrid car to reduce their own carbon dioxide (CO_2) emissions.

I have spent the bulk of my professional career as a journalist covering the global automotive industry. From 2006 to 2007, I wrote a series of columns that ran in the evening edition of the *Nihon Keizai Shimbun* business newspaper entitled "Clean Car

Wars." This book is a compilation of the topics I covered during that time. In it, I attempt to provide an overview of the different technologies and forces that are driving the auto industry toward greener pastures, and what it will take to survive into the twenty-first century. I place particular emphasis on describing initiatives by the "Big Three" Japanese automakers in this realm, namely Toyota, Honda, and Nissan, but also try to highlight the efforts of auto companies in the U.S. and Europe as well. I also felt compelled to delve into the histories of Toyota and Honda to shed some light on the various factors and decisions that have led them to where they are today, including a concluding description of the management philosophies that have helped put Toyota and Honda slightly ahead of the environmental technology curve.

In short, I have tried to provide what I believe is a glimpse into various possible trajectories for the auto industry. Nearly every path leads away from fossil fuels, but is there a right or true path? And if so, who is on it?

Finally, I would like to express my sincerest gratitude to Nick Wallwork, Janis Soo, Joel Balbin, Fiona Wong, David Rule, Ian Rowley and all those who helped in the behind-the-scenes creation of this book, with a particular shout-out to Mitsuru Mabuchi, who provided invaluable translation assistance.

Yozo Hasegawa
November 2007

Introduction

Green Technology to Drive Market Dominance

The Yaegashi Bond Shock

When the Standard & Poor's rating agency downgraded General Motors Corp. (GM) and Ford Motor Co. to junk-bond status in May 2005, the Civil Society Institute (CSI), a U.S. nonprofit organization committed to promoting high fuel-efficiency standards for cars sold in the U.S., issued a statement saying new debt issued by the faltering American auto giants should be called "Yaegashi bonds."

"Yaegashi" referred to Takehisa Yaegashi, a Toyota Motor Corp. engineer who played an instrumental role in the Japanese car-maker's hybrid-technology project. For Pam Solo, the president of the CSI, Yaegashi personifies a key strategic difference between Japanese and American auto manufacturers: an early commitment to the development of cleaner-running cars.

In September 2006, California's judicial authorities sued six U.S. and Japanese automakers over environmental damage caused by the emissions of the vehicles they make. The suit, filed in the U.S. District Court in northern California, accused the top U.S. and Japanese manufacturers of contributing to global warming, which was causing significant harm to the state's environment and economy, and demanded that they pay for the damage. It was the first attempt by

U.S. authorities to hold automakers accountable for the greenhouse gases their products emit. Claiming that the state was suffering damages totaling tens of millions of dollars due to the emissions of their vehicles, Bill Lockyer, then state's attorney-general, placed the onus on car manufacturers to improve their environmental performance.

One prominent American environmental evangelist closely monitoring the auto industry is Amory Lovins, chairman and chief scientist of Rocky Mountain Institute, a nonprofit organization providing consultancy on energy matters. Traveling across the world, Lovins has been preaching the gospel of efficient energy use, which he says is crucial for global economic growth as well as environmental protection.

At a symposium on the issue of global sustainability held at the University of Tokyo in February 2006, Lovins noted that fuel efficiency in cars held the key to the environmental health of the planet. Automobiles account for 70 percent of oil consumption in the U.S., he pointed out. Lovins lauded Japanese car manufacturers for their efforts on this front, saying that companies such as Toyota, Nissan Motor Co., Ltd., and Honda Motor Co. were firmly committed to improving the energy efficiency of their products, striving to achieve their own specific targets for cutting CO_2 emissions.

Also in attendance at the symposium was Takamitsu Sawa, director of the Institute of Economic Research of Kyoto University, who argued that the question of how to deal with the challenge of global warming is what has triggered realignment in the auto industry. His comments were supported by the president of the University of Tokyo, Hiroshi Komiyama, who maintained that meeting the challenge of global sustainability will require at least a trebling of energy efficiency, doubling the use of renewable energy sources and establishing a global material-recycling system by 2050.

"A worldwide switch to hybrid cars would reduce gasoline consumption by two-thirds immediately."

Toyota in the Hybrid Driver's Seat

The North American International Auto Show is held every January in Detroit, Michigan. It is considered the most important car event in the world, and takes place in the heart of the world's biggest auto market. What has traditionally been a gala celebration to show off the fastest, sleekest, and most powerful automotive concepts that human engineering can muster is rapidly shaping into a battle over concepts and technologies that emphasize efficiency, conservation, and sustainability. At the 2007 event, every major car manufacturer weighed in with deep-pocketed advertising campaigns designed to convince the world that they had seen the future, and that it was green. For some, that future was now. For others, it was still a good ten years away. Needless to say, the claims were all being shaped by soaring oil prices, tightening environmental regulations, disgruntled consumers, and growing concerns about global warming.

Toyota proved that the future could be both clean and sexy, unveiling a seductive-looking FT-HS Hybrid Sports Concept that boasted all the super-low emissions and fuel efficiency of a hybrid car with the essential trappings of a sports car, including a powerful V6, 3.5-liter engine. Building on its success with the Prius, the first successfully mass-produced hybrid car, Toyota was looking to maintain its edge by taking its green-car initiative to the next logical step.

Toyota FT-HS Hybrid Sports
Photograph courtesy of Toyota Motor Corp.

In 2006, Toyota sold 192,000 hybrid cars in the U.S., and is counting on a 50 percent increase to 300,000 units in 2007. In Detroit, the president of Toyota Motor North America, Inc., Jim Press (now with Chrysler LLC), exemplified the company's sense of vigilance by referring to the old adage that staying on top is always more difficult than getting there. Indeed, Toyota in 2006 continued to encroach upon Big Three (GM, Ford, and Chrysler) territory in terms of new car sales, sliding into the number three slot behind GM and Ford. The success of Toyota's bid to vie with GM for most auto sales in the world began to look more and more like a foregone conclusion, with projections that the Japanese automaker would shatter the nine million sales mark in 2007. Indeed, this was borne out in late April, when early reports of fiscal 2007 results indicated that Toyota had indeed overtaken GM in the first quarter of the calendar year to become the world's biggest auto company.

Toyota president Katsuaki Watanabe said immediately after assuming the company helm in 2005 that he would seek to increase global sales of hybrid cars to one million early in the second decade of the twenty-first century by building on the strong "green" image the company was earning with the Prius, thanks in large part to a growing legion of Hollywood stars, such as Leonardo di Caprio, who were snapping

Lexus LS 600hL hybrid
Photograph courtesy of Toyota Motor Corp.

up the vehicle and, thereby, doing Toyota's PR work. Watanabe wanted to begin rolling out complete hybrid systems in as many vehicle models as possible, in addition to the Prius, and called upon all group companies to do their part in a global campaign to make the word "environmental" synonymous with "Toyota."

The previous year in Detroit, Toyota had unveiled a hybrid version of its best-selling U.S. car, the Camry saloon, and announced that it would offer a prestige hybrid version of a top-of-the-line Lexus luxury sedan, the LS 460, in early 2007. The hybrid was later retagged the LS 600h L and dubbed "the world's most advanced luxury sedan."

In China, Toyota began production of the Prius at the end of 2005, and followed in October 2006 with

2006 Prius from China
Photograph courtesy of Toyota Motor Corp.

production of a hybrid Camry in Georgetown, Kentucky. Whereas Toyota had previously felt the need to keep its hybrid production close to its chest in Japan, due to many proprietary patents, that hybrid production has begun moving overseas indicates that the company has entered a new phase in its hybrid-rollout strategy.

The Prius is now being assembled in China, but because basic components still have to be imported from Japan, the vehicle is slapped with the same 26 percent tariff as finished imports. As a result, it carries a whopping sticker price of 288,000 renminbi (about US$35,000). In North America, meanwhile, Toyota plans to produce about 48,000 hybrid Camrys a year, more than 10 percent of its annual North American auto sales of 400,000.

Sales of the Prius in North America began in 2000. Seven years later, the gasoline-electric vehicle accounted for nearly half of all hybrids sold in the U.S. But in an age in which American consumers are again opting for higher fuel efficiency in the face of high prices at the pump and fears of global warming, Toyota's current strategy is to push its hybrid technology across its entire fleet, erasing the niche-segment distinction and earning the hybrid "full citizenship" status.

A Presence in Every Market, Every Segment

The Prius is, however, only part of Toyota's surge. The enormous company's product line is bulging with a diverse array of hot-selling vehicles, from the diminutive Yaris and other fuel-efficient subcompacts to the mainstay Camry sedan, and of course, the Lexus brand. Even without the Prius, Toyota sales have been brisk in North America, a market that accounts for more than 60 percent of Toyota's global profits.

Three months into 2006, Toyota passed Ford to rank second in the U.S., in terms of new car sales, behind GM, bumping DaimlerChrysler out of the "top three" category for the first time.

Toyota also used the 2007 Detroit Auto Show to roll out its largest Tundra, a beefy pickup truck that demonstrated Toyota's aims at a market segment still dominated by Detroit brands. The move may have backfired, however, because environmentalists lambasted Toyota for its "hypocrisy."

"Building Priuses does not give Toyota license to mass-produce the Tundra," said Sarah Connolly, co-director of the Freedom from Oil Campaign for Rainforest Action Network.

But Toyota has a stated objective of wielding a strong presence in all markets and across all automobile segments. At the 2006 Paris Motor Show, for example, Toyota launched its next-generation RAV4—the most popular sports utility vehicle (SUV) in Europe and Toyota's cash cow in that market. The RAV4 created a sensation after its debut in 1994, giving consumers the benefits of an SUV, but in a smaller, more fuel-efficient package. Toyota's compacts and ultra-compacts also do well in Europe, prompting industry observers to project that Toyota's next big battle in Europe will be over the luxury car segment, and signaling a head-on clash between Mercedes and Lexus.

2006 RAV4
Photograph courtesy of Toyota Motor Corp.

Europe has also been shifting to diesel vehicles ever since the European Commission lowered taxes on diesel fuel, which is more fuel-efficient and burns less CO_2 than regular gasoline. Although the market for diesel cars has been almost non-existent in Japan and North America, Toyota realizes its significance in Europe. In November 2006, Toyota forged a strategic alliance with Isuzu Motors, Japan's second-largest truck maker, with a strong track record in diesel-engine technology. Diesel technology is also advancing quickly to the point where it may rival hybrids as a green alternative in the near and distant future. Toyota is banking on Isuzu to help ramp up its diesel portfolio quickly, in addition to incorporating diesel into its overall green-car strategy.

"Since we are developing environmental technologies and products in a variety of fields, it was clear that we needed to enhance our diesel line as well," remarked Toyota president Watanabe, sitting alongside Isuzu president Yoshinori Ida at a press conference to announce the tie-up.

Toyota's strategic focus on green technologies is founded upon the recognition that automakers must reduce the environmental impact of their products if they ever hope to lead their field in the twenty-first century. So maintaining its reputation as the greenest car company in the world is intricately tied to being the greatest car company in the world. But as Press was quick to allude, there's always someone ready to knock you off your pedestal.

It's no accident that the closest competitor in Toyota's rear-view mirror is another Japanese company. The fuel-economy ratings for 2007 models released by the U.S. Department of Energy and the Environmental Protection Agency (EPA), in October 2006, strongly demonstrated the mileage superiority of Japanese-engineered hybrid technology. The list of cars that get the best mileage was topped by the Toyota Prius, followed by the Honda Civic Hybrid and Toyota Camry Hybrid. Hybrid vehicles generally get better mileage in city streets than purely gas-powered cars. According to the EPA data, the Prius gets 60 miles per gallon in the city, and 51 on the highway. Among American auto companies, the Ford Escape Hybrid, released in 2004, performed best, ranking fourth overall.

Honda's Attacks on Two Fronts: Hybrid and Diesel

Toyota's hybrid success with the Prius left Honda chomping at the bit and feeling upstaged. When Takeo Fukui became president of Honda in 2003, he raised the banner of "returning to the riverhead of Honda's management," which essentially meant regaining that technological edge and esprit de corps that had always made Honda a leader, not a follower, particularly in the realm of energy efficiency.

So at the Detroit Auto Show, when Honda unveiled its next-generation concept car, the FCX—a hydrogen fuel-cell vehicle that "drives completely clean," and announced that it would start shipping in 2008—the company that is

Honda FCX
Photograph courtesy of Honda Motor Co.

capable of inspiring a cultlike devotion to its products around the world showed itself eager to raise the ante in the green car war.

Toyota and Honda both began their initiatives to develop hybrid systems at about the same time in the early 1990s. Toyota was the first to bring a hybrid vehicle to the market, with its 1997 launch of the 1.5-liter Prius. Two years later in 1999, Honda began selling the Insight, a smaller, two-passenger hybrid with a three-cylinder, one-liter engine. In contrast to Toyota's hybrid system, which used specially designed high-powered motors, Honda's system involved a motor that worked more as an assist device integrated

Honda Insight
Photograph courtesy of Honda Motor Co.

with a gasoline engine. As a result, Honda was able to come out with a hybrid system that was far more compact than that of Toyota. Moreover, Honda released the Insight in the U.S. ahead of the Toyota Prius, making the Insight, not the Prius, the first mass-produced hybrid car sold in the U.S.

Honda received the boost it was looking for at the 2006 Detroit Auto Show when it garnered both the "North American Car of the Year" and "North American Truck of the Year" awards, and then proceeded to unveil a fully remodeled Civic and a Civic Hybrid to prove that it was keeping pace with Toyota. Honda walked away leaving everyone with a clear impression that the focus of its hybrid strategy was not only on lowering emissions and raising fuel efficiency, but also on mak-

Civic Hybrid
Photograph courtesy of Honda Motor Co.

ing the hybrid much more accessible. At the 2006 Paris Motor Show, Honda pre-empted a Japan debut by showing off its new model, mid-size SUV, the CR-V, in response to the consumer shift in Europe away from small cars to compact, or crossover, SUVs. Honda prepared both two-liter gasoline and 2.4-liter diesel-engine versions.

Fukui has for years preached the importance of making hybrid systems smaller and lighter for deployment in compact, lower-priced vehicles, repeatedly stating that only when the price differential between hybrid and gasoline vehicles have been reduced to less than 200,000 yen (US$1,700), will they truly come into widespread use. Smaller and cheaper hybrids seem destined to play a larger role in Honda's comeback strategy.

Europe and the Big Three Respond

In 2006, while Japanese manufacturers were reaching all-time highs in U.S. market share for auto sales at a combined 34.8 percent, the Big Three American automakers had plummeted to an all-time low of 53.7 percent. But turnarounds are common in this industry, and the Big Three still wield plenty of muscle and desire. Along with hammering out a first-phase restructuring plan to streamline and strengthen their operations, U.S. automakers have come out swinging, with a variety of environmental strategies of their own.

At the 2007 Detroit Auto Show, GM chairman Richard Wagoner emphasized his company's drive to develop automobiles that can adapt to the diversity of energy sources that will become available in the future, be it gasoline, ethanol, hydrogen, solar power, or any number of alternatives depending on availability in each region or country. GM then announced the "E-Flex"

Chevrolet Volt
Photography courtesy of © GM Corp. This image is licensed under Creative Commons 3.0 License.

platform, a new vehicle architecture designed to convert a variety of fuels into electric power. GM also unveiled an electric automobile concept called the "Chevrolet Volt," which houses a lithium-ion battery that can be recharged at home. It is due out in 2010.

Ford countered by announcing its own "plug-in" hybrid system, with a concept car dubbed "Airstream," which combines hybrid and fuel-cell technologies.

Until Daimler spun off Chrysler in May 2007, DaimlerChrysler, had also been forging ahead under charismatic chairman Dieter Zetsche, with an environmental strategy that was patently

European. Zetsche pointed to the brilliant performance of DaimlerChrysler's "BlueTec," a powerful, economical, and clean diesel-drive system, which reduces NO_x emissions.

Europe's leading automakers are all staking their futures on clean-burning diesel engines as the mainstream green technology for automobiles. By boldly declaring early achievability of new U.S. emissions standards that are slated to go into effect in 2009, Zetsche cleverly presented DaimlerChrysler as a company that is already a step ahead of the environmental curve.

Sporting his trademark Kaiser moustache, Zetsche beamed confidently on stage in Detroit, saying that a clean-running diesel engine should find a warm welcome in the U.S. and Japan. When queried about Chrysler's drop in revenue for fiscal 2006, the first year of his tenure as chairman, Zetsche responded cheerfully: "We're off to a great start in 2007."

Zetsche took a hatchet to the slumping Chrysler group during the confusion immediately after the merger between Daimler-Benz and Chrysler, and brought the division back to profitability in 2005, largely due to the success of the full-size luxury sedan, Chrysler 300C. Those results helped seal his future as the successor to then company head Jurgen Schrempp. But soon after taking office, oil prices skyrocketed, sending the Chrysler group back into the red, and exposing the company's over-reliance on sales of gas-guzzling trucks and SUVs. Although DaimlerChrysler overall came out ahead in 2006 thanks to strong earnings and the return to growth of its Mercedes car group, the Chrysler group's red ink prompted consideration of a drastic reform plan.

The reform effort included a decision by Zetsche to spin off the North American Chrysler division, and in May 2007, he announced the sale of that division to American asset-management firm Cerberus Capital Management. Upon disposing of a division that sells an annual 2.65 million cars, the company returned to being just "Daimler," a move that rapidly improved its balance sheet, even while it meant a large drop in aggregate sales volume. After the purchase, Cerberus chairman John W. Snow moved to assure investors and the public that "our involvement is for the long term," in hopes of quelling speculation of a quick sell-off, and exhibiting a resolve to strengthen Chrysler's management team. But due to the difficulties expected in engineering a rapid earnings recovery, rumors about a possible turnaround sale to an emerging-country player such as a Korean or Chinese company continue.

European automakers such as Volkswagen AG (VW) of Germany and France's PSA Peugeot Citroen S.A., too, are having to revamp their earnings regimes in the face of escalating raw material costs, stricter environmental regulations and, to a certain degree, the success of Japanese competitors.

The shakeup at VW, Europe's biggest carmaker, was initiated by its former chairman and CEO, Ferdinand Piech, now chairman of the supervisory board, and the man credited for turning VW around in North America with the new Beetle. As the grandson of Dr. Ferdinand Porsche, best known for designing the original VW Beetle, Piech is a major shareholder in Porsche, and co-developed some of its most popular models. So when in the autumn of 2005, Porsche became the leading shareholder of VW, management was solidified under Piech. As 2006 drew to a close, Piech suddenly removed the man he had recruited for the job of CEO, former Bavarian Motor Works AG (BMW) head Dr. Bernd Pischetsrieder. That was then followed by the January 2007 departure of the group's number two man in Wolfgang Bernhardt, who headed the VW brand. Coming in to take over was Martin Winterkorn, who had been CEO of VW's subsidiary Audi brand, and in whom Pischetsrieder was said to harbor great confidence as the one eventually to succeed him at the helm of VW.

At Peugeot Citroen, Jean-Martin Folz announced his surprise early retirement in 2007 after serving as chief executive for nine years. Similarly, at BMW, Helmut Panke, who since 2002 had been the luxury carmaker's chairman, also retired, citing the company's mandatory retirement age of 60. Panke had orchestrated the group's growth from annual sales of a million units to 1.3 million units during his tenure. Nevertheless, in September of 2006, Panke was succeeded by production chief Norbert Reithofer, a man ten years his junior.

No one has been faster to the mark in Europe than French automaker, Renault S.A., which welcomed Nissan's CEO, Carlos Ghosn, back to France to double as Renault CEO. In February 2006, the French group announced its "Commitment 2009" to shift management emphasis over to earnings, rather than sales volume. Nissan has been a strong contributor to Renault's bottom line, but with operating profits projected to decrease at Nissan for the first time since the Ghosn era began—owing to slumping demand and a host of other factors—the aura of infallibility that had surrounded the hardworking and charismatic CEO is in jeopardy. Ghosn plans to overcome this latest challenge, however, with a stronger emphasis on Nissan's minicar line and more investment in new models. "There will be a few ups and downs, but the Renault–Nissan alliance will continue to grow," Ghosn remarked at the Detroit Auto Show.

Although most European automakers struggle in their home markets, veteran Italian automaker Fiat S.p.A. seems to be the lone winner, closing out fiscal 2006 with double-digit increases in profits and revenues. The Italian brand dissolved its five-year capital and business tie-up with GM, and brought in industry outsider Sergio Marchionne to head up a rebuilding drive that looks to have paid off handsomely. Marchionne changed the inward-looking attitude of the company, and successfully engineered a new corporate culture that seems to thrive on competition.

But without question, the major management shakeup taking place across all of Europe's major automakers has been motivated by a desire to rebuild competitiveness in time to gain ground on environment and fuel-efficiency leaders such as Toyota and Honda. For many of them, the best prospect for bridging the gap seems to lie in the diesel engine. Diesel-powered cars constitute more than half of all new vehicle sales in Europe, and have become the de facto "eco-car" of Europe.

GM Holds Its Ground

By the time the Detroit Auto Show rolled around in 2007, GM had proven it still possessed the fundamental strengths to remain atop the auto industry. Although poor sales had swollen the company's loss sheets, a much-needed reorganization was taking place. GM shed some of its workforce through voluntary early retirement, closed down plants, spun off its financial-services subsidiary, and dissolved its capital tie-ups with Fuji Heavy Industries Ltd. and Isuzu Motors. As a result, GM was able to get over the liquidity crunch that had plagued it. By 2006, the teetering auto giant had succeeded in drastically reducing its deficit, and was at work pounding out an aggressive growth strategy.

In June, 2006, GM chairman and CEO Wagoner received a letter from Tracinda Corp., an investment firm interested in speeding up GM's recovery, run by billionaire mogul Kirk Kerkorian. As the third-largest shareholder in GM, Kerkorian was hoping to bring about a landmark alliance between GM and Ghosn's Renault and Nissan, which would see Renault and Nissan purchase a significant stake in GM, and bring the number one automaker into their fold. But four months later in October, Wagoner nixed the proposal, much to Kerkorian's dismay, saying essentially that GM wanted to rebuild on its own, and that Renault–

Chevrolet Sequel
Photography courtesy of © GM Corp. This image is licensed under Creative Commons 3.0 License.

Nissan would have much more to gain than GM from the venture. The following month, Wagoner then flew to Shanghai—where GM is the undisputed champion in auto sales—and took part in a ceremonial test drive of the Chevrolet Sequel, a hydrogen fuel-cell-powered SUV that uses no gasoline. GM still had its swagger.

After drawing attention to its dominance in the Chinese market, Wagoner then made a brief stop in Japan, where he called on Toyota president Watanabe to touch base on their existing partnerships, and talk about some possible new ones. Wagoner also took the opportunity to meet with Yoshinori Ida, president of Isuzu, for the first time since selling off its stake in the Japanese automaker. He then paid a visit to Osamu Suzuki, chairman and chief executive of Suzuki Motor Corp., with which GM had a long and fruitful strategic relationship; that is, until their recent necessity-driven divestiture.

Not failing to seize the moment, however, Toyota stepped into the spot vacated by GM, and purchased a large stake in Isuzu, forming a business tie-up to cooperate in the development of small diesel engines for passenger cars. The move was testament to Toyota's need to increase its partnerships with other Japanese firms in an age of escalating oil prices and R&D costs, something it had hitherto disdained.

GM had already teamed up with two German carmakers, Daimler and BMW, in the development of hybrid systems. At the 2006 Detroit Auto Show, rather than address the firm's current financial morass, Wagoner chose to speak in rosy terms about new business prospects in this sphere, alluding to the development of a revolutionary "dual-mode hybrid system" as early fruits of the three-party alliance. Wagoner predicted that there would be more partnerships in environmental technology of this nature to come. Just how GM develops and implements its fuel-cell initiatives, such as the Sequel and its E-Flex platform, should prove critical to its resurgence as the world's automotive leader.

Although Wagoner had succeeded in resisting a potentially historic alliance, he remains a believer in the inevitability of further consolidation. GM just needs to do it on its own terms. As with Toyota's motivations for partnering with Isuzu, Wagoner commented that the rising cost of materials and technology keeps thoughts of consolidation on everyone's minds. A merger on the scale of the now defunct DaimlerChrysler union in 1998 seems likely to happen again.

Ford Embraces Environmentalism

Another iconic American auto company faced many of the same challenges as GM: red ink, slumping sales, and a dire need for reorganization. In September 2006, Ford recruited The Boeing Company vice president Alan Mulally to pilot the company as its new president and CEO. The appointment came from executive chairman William Clay Ford Jr., the great-grandson of company founder Henry Ford. As chairman of the board, Ford Jr. had been dreaming of restoring the Ford family cachet, and became CEO in October 2001, after the company's poor performance led to the dismissal of CEO Jacques Nasser. Although Ford Jr. managed to put the brakes on Ford's decline, fortunes began to sour again in the latter part of his five-year stint, and Ford's percentage of new auto sales in the U.S. plummeted from the upper twenties to the mid-teens.

As point man for the commercial airplane division of Boeing, Mulally had demonstrated a shrewd talent for cost-cutting and business turnarounds. At the press conference to announce the change in Ford's leadership, Mulally confidently hinted at an overhaul of the company's product lineup, especially in the area of large vehicles such as pickups and SUVs.

Three months later in December, Mulally made a secret trip to Japan, and met with Toyota chairman Fujio Cho. Early in 2007, he also made the rounds to GM, Chrysler, and BMW, generating speculation among industry observers about a possible global consolidation in the works.

Ford Jr., is a self-proclaimed environmentalist, and has personally sought to boost Ford's eco-image by bringing to market alternative fuel or hybrid vehicles. With a 33.4 percent stake in Mazda Motor Corp., Ford has also been looking to strengthen its partnership with its Japanese affiliate, particularly in the small-car space. This has been accompanied by the rise of Ford executive vice president, Mark Fields, who served Mazda as its president and CEO from 1999 to 2002. Mazda has also been making a name for itself in environmental R&D, having succeeded in fusing its famous rotary engine with a hydrogen-powered system. Mazda wields enough environmental muscle to survive on its own should it ever depart from the Ford group.

Soon after the U.S. congressional midterm elections ended in defeat for the Republican party in November 2006, President Bush met with the leaders of the Big Three automakers, and urged them to voluntarily begin building the infrastructure for plug-in hybrids and ethanol-blended fuel vehicles. But they may not have needed the prodding. With Toyota and Honda looking to corner the market in "green, fuel-efficient" cars for the future, GM and Ford wasted no time in responding with strong new initiatives of their own at the 2007 Detroit Auto Show, even though both companies already had fairly successful hybrid vehicles on the road already: the Escape Hybrid and Mercury Mariner Hybrid for Ford, and the Silverado and GMC Sierra hybrid pickups for Chevrolet. But while Toyota and Honda, by 2007, seemed to have established a lock on the hybrid market with their crossbreed versions of the Toyota Prius, Camry, and Highlander; and the Honda Insight and Accord, this was just the first salvo in what is sure to become a protracted

2008 Ford Escape Hybrid
Photograph courtesy of Ford Motor Company.
This image is licensed under Creative
Commons Attribution 2.0 License.

competition for next-generation technologies leading the automotive industry away from carbon-based fuels. Growing apprehensions about the immediate effects of global warming, the potential for widening conflict and instability in the oil-producing Middle East, and, of course, the relatively surprising commercial success of hybrid vehicles, had made this very clear.

Chapter 1

Toyota Launches the Hybrid Age

The Twenty-First-Century Passenger Car

In April 2007, Toyota surpassed GM as the biggest auto company in the world in both production and sales for at least the first quarter.

"We're concerned with performance. We're not really thinking about becoming the world's biggest auto company," said Toyota president Katsuaki Watanabe. "We won't see growth without improving quality, so it's of the utmost importance that we be leaders in technology and manufacturing. That's what will earn the support of our customers."

While Watanabe sought to downplay the perceived historical significance of the feat, it was the main topic of discussion among journalists and attendees of the annual year-end press conference he gave in Nagoya on December 23, 2006. The speculation was triggered by an announcement of a production and sales plan made three months earlier at the regular executive board meeting on September 20, which forecast that Toyota's consolidated sales worldwide for fiscal 2007, including those for group brands Daihatsu Motor Co. and Hino Motors, would rise 6 percent and surpass the nine million mark for the first time in the company's history, reaching 9,340,000 vehicles sold.

"We're projecting consolidated global sales of 9.8 million units in 2008," Watanabe glowed. "We aim to strengthen our footprint and secure sustained growth."

The meeting took place, as it always does, at the Royal Park Hotel in Tokyo's venerated Suitengu district, where a large screen projected Toyota's spiking sales figures from 8.13 million vehicles in 2005, up more than 20 percent to 8.85 million units in 2006.

"We can't expect to grow, however, without constant qualitative improvements," Watanabe added. "We must be honest, thorough, and diligent." These are words often used to describe Watanabe himself and his proven ability to get things done through hard work and persistence.

"Let's not fool ourselves in expecting oil prices to return to past levels," added executive vice president Kazuo Okamoto. "We need to continue to strengthen our efforts at reducing costs, improving our engines and fuel efficiency, and securing our competitive edge with the rapid deployment of our hybrid technology."

The list of tasks laid out by top management was long. First, in the area of alternative automotive fuels, there was bioethanol made from low CO_2-emitting biomass materials. Okamoto was quick to point out that Toyota has already made every vehicle it produces capable of running on E10 fuel, a 90 percent–10 percent blend of gasoline and ethanol. He also drew attention to several joint research projects under way, one to develop fuel based on hydrogenated vegetable oil with the Nippon Oil Corporation, and another launched with Shell Gas & Power to develop a biodiesel fuel called FT (Fischer–Tropsch), which converts natural gas to liquid and burns cleanly. In late 2002, Toyota also became the first auto company in the world to begin leasing hydrogen fuel-cell vehicles with zero emissions.

But it was the announcement of planned research into PHEV technology, a zero-emissions electric vehicle, which garnered significant attention at the meeting. The PHEV houses a battery that can be recharged in the home, using household electrical sources, and is a fusion of electrical and gas power. With a larger battery, one can choose to power the vehicle either through its combustion engine or its electrical motor, depending on the driving situation. In the city and over short distances, the vehicle would run as an electric car, but then shift to hybrid power generation for medium-to-longer distances, cutting current hybrid-vehicle fuel consumption nearly in half.

The spotlight shone brightly on the plug-in hybrid in the U.S. during President Bush's State of the Union address to Congress on January 31, 2006, when he outlined his Advanced Energy Initiative. Stressing the importance of diversifying energy sources and developing more efficient vehicles, the president promised redoubled R&D efforts in hybrid vehicle and plug-in hybrid battery technology. "Accelerated consumer adoption of hybrid-electric vehicles offers the potential to significantly reduce oil consumption in the near term," Bush stated in "The President's Energy Vision". "Plug-in hybrids would generally be charged at night, when electric utilities have spare generating capacity available."

Although this may have sounded like a new proposal to many Americans, it struck many Toyota watchers as indirect acknowledgment of Toyota's lead in environmental technology.

Toyota, of course, isn't anywhere near ready to fully replace cost-efficient gasoline with alternative fuels. But until the switch can be made, hybrid technology will continue to serve as the leading contributor to fuel-efficiency improvements, and can be applied to every type of power train. Toyota therefore remains committed to advancing its gasoline-hybrid and diesel-hybrid programs.

Toyota Acquires Isuzu

On November 7, 2006, Toyota acquired a 5.9 percent stake in Isuzu, and announced joint development and production of fuel-efficient diesel engines. That same afternoon, Toyota revealed its half-year results, which included profits up 35 percent to more than a trillion yen (about $9.5 billion) for the very first time, leading to projections that Toyota would finish the fiscal year in March with operating profits up 17 percent for the year at 2.2 trillion yen (about $19 billion), breaking the two trillion mark for the first time. On the strength of these results, Toyota was able to confidently announce its tie-up with Isuzu that very evening, a partnership that immediately gave Toyota world-class diesel-engine technology, and boosted its domestic leadership in trucks.

Toyota has Japan's largest truckmaker, Hino Motors, as one of its subsidiaries. But on a worldwide basis, Daimler is king, and commands a growing lead. In 2006, as part of its revival plan, GM decided to dissolve the capital tie-up it had enjoyed with Isuzu since 1971, allowing the conventionally go-it-alone Toyota to seize upon a once-in-a-lifetime opportunity. Although Isuzu had lost a stable shareholder in GM, giant Japanese trading companies in the form of Mitsubishi and Itochu corporations materialized to pick up the freed-up stock.

GM has been working with Toyota since 1984 through their joint venture, New United Motor Manufacturing, Inc. (NUMMI), a huge auto-manufacturing plant in Fremont, California. With Isuzu, GM had established a joint venture company in diesel-engine production in the U.S. and in Poland. Toyota knew that timing was important once GM stepped away, and quickly saw an injection of capital into Isuzu as a grand opportunity to strengthen its truck division without provoking GM.

"Diesel engines are important to keeping us competitive in the European market," commented Watanabe at his press conference with Ida to announce the tie-up. "With Isuzu, we supplement our technology, and garner great possibilities in advanced engine development for both parties." Clearly, the role of diesel technology in achieving mastery of the automotive universe, particularly in Europe, was not lost on the Toyota chief. In addition to collaborating on the design and production of diesel engines for small passenger cars, the two Japanese automakers plan to co-develop diesel-engine exhaust-control systems, along with a broad range of environmental technologies that include basic engine technology and alternative fuels, hopefully bringing to market a jointly developed diesel car within three years.

Moreover, Isuzu's diesel know-how is not confined to trucks. Isuzu produces a wide variety of diesel engines, from 1,700cc to 6,600cc classes, and has the proud distinction of having been the first in Japan to develop a diesel-engine passenger car. The often-overshadowed Japanese maker also boasts an established reputation as a leader in low-fuel-consumption, environmentally friendly technologies. Indeed, Isuzu diesel engines can be found powering cars all around the world, including those built by GM and Renault. Toyota believes it is capable of effectively incorporating Isuzu's advanced diesel-engine technology, rather than relying solely on internal development.

With Hino as its subsidiary, Toyota records the highest domestic sales of midsize-to-large commercial trucks. But perched atop that sector, as of 2005, was Daimler, followed by the Swedish automaker, AB Volvo, under the Renault group. Hino falls much further below in the rankings. But by bringing Isuzu, as Japan's number two truckmaker, under its wing, Toyota gains a powerful foothold in a market where its presence has traditionally been weak.

Europe Banks on Diesel

Diesel vehicles have suffered from a bad image in Japan, and have been saddled with heavy restrictions. This is why Toyota has balked at manufacturing all but a few diesel-powered passenger cars. But in Europe, where the market for diesel vehicles continues to grow, Toyota is actively involved in

Toyota Avensis diesel
Photograph courtesy of Toyota Motor Corp.

diesel development, running an exclusive diesel-engine plant in Poland, for example, to power its Europe-targeted car, the Avensis.

A huge billboard at France's Nice Airport draws attention to "Clean Power. Toyota's unique diesel," and Toyota doubled its sales of diesel cars in Europe from 540,000 vehicles in 1998 to more than a million in 2006, breaking the million mark for the first time. Diesel cars account for more than 40 percent of Toyota's European offerings.

Perhaps most striking about Toyota's long-term strategy is that it is founded upon a two-pronged, tactical blitz to cover the globe with every sort of vehicle imaginable, and across every category. Buoyed by the continued growth of the automotive market around the world, Toyota is ramping up production in the premium-brand, middle-class, and compact-car segments, while continuously looking for new ways to streamline its hallowed manufacturing processes. Financially, it is a policy that aims to elevate Toyota's consolidated income-to-sales ratio from 8.9 percent (in fiscal 2006) up and over the 10 percent plateau. Among them, the eco-car as represented by its hybrids plays a heavy-hitting role in creating a favorable image for the company. And now that hybrid strategy has been extended to Lexus, Toyota's exceedingly successful foray into the luxury-car market that began in the U.S. in 1989.

The Lexus brand was brought to Japan in 2005, starting with sales of the Lexus GS (formerly the Toyota Alisto), the IS (formerly the Toyota Altezza), and the SC (formerly the Toyota Soarer). In September 2006, the company's flagship sedan, the new LS 460, was added to round out the Lexus lineup in Toyota's home market. To emphasize its luxury status, the Lexus LS was unveiled against the sleek, whitewashed façade of the New National Theater, Tokyo in the fashionable Shibuya district. White is the most popular color for cars in Japan, and evokes a sense of class and sophistication. Toyota succeeded in generating excitement over the LS with its four- and six-liter, V8 engine and world's first computerized control, eight-speed automatic transmission. In addition to offering power and fuel efficiency, the LS is capable of detecting and signaling to the driver the presence of other vehicles, pedestrians, or obstructions, and comes equipped with warning sensors that detect when a vehicle approaches too close from the rear.

A prototype Lexus LS 460 hybrid was also shown to underscore Toyota's commitment to extending its hybrid technology to all of its brands. Toyota hopes to increase Lexus sales from 470,000 units in 2006 to more than 500,000 in 2007. Retailing at between 7.7 million yen and 9.65 million yen (US$66,000–US$83,500), the LS 460 is being counted upon to raise Toyota margins significantly.

At a press conference immediately after the declaration that Toyota would sell 9.8 million vehicles worldwide in 2008, Toyota chairman and Japan Automobile Manufacturing Association Council chairman Fujio Cho was quick to insert a qualifier. "In an arena where competition takes place on a global scale, overly optimistic forecasts are taboo," he said. "But I can say that technology will be what produces winners in this field—particularly environmental technology. The automobile still offers enormous room for improvement, but that can only be accomplished through capital investment. To be globally competitive, it is imperative that we put in place in Japan a strong system for supporting and promoting joint R&D efforts among private industry and academic institutions, at the same level of intensity and commitment as is seen abroad."

Sakichi Toyoda's Challenge

The Prius, on its arrival, achieved what it originally set out to do: set the standard for a mass-produced passenger car of the twenty-first century. But to understand how Toyota's hybrid program came about, one really has to travel back to the birth of the Japanese auto industry itself, and to the words of Sakichi Toyoda, inventor of Japan's first automatic power loom, founder of Toyota Industries Corporation, and father to Toyota founder Kiichiro Toyoda.

> You can build the best automobile or airplane ever made, yet you still need petroleum for its propulsion. Ours is a nation that must rely completely on imports for that resource. But where we are helplessly poor in petroleum, we are rich in hydropower. If we can turn that abundant resource into electricity, we can reduce our dependence on outside sources. We can power automobiles and airplanes. To accomplish this, however, we need to develop a battery that can generate high voltage, be durable, and quickly rechargeable; a battery that loses very little of its charge naturally, and meets with minimal internal resistance. It must also be simple and compact in design and construction.

It was a stiff challenge, but Sakichi Toyoda had every reason to believe that such an innovation was possible. He knew that researchers in such far-flung places as Moscow and the Edison

Laboratory in Menlo Park, California, were already hard at work on similar issues. So Sakichi decided to hold a contest in October 1925, and offer a prize of a million yen to anyone who could develop the world's best "electrical storage device." The contest was held under government auspices through the Imperial Institute of Invention and Innovation (renamed the Japan Institute of Invention and Innovation in 1947), a body organized to protect industrial property and promote inventions.

The contest committee comprised Japan's leading physicists and electrochemists, including its most renowned atomic physicist, Hantaro Nagaoka. A special facility dubbed the "Toyoda Research Lab" was set up exclusively for battery technology development

Sakichi Toyoda
Photograph courtesy of Toyota Motor Corp.

by the Institute of Invention and Innovation. A great many scientists, scholars, and engineers from many academic disciplines were brought in to tackle the problem, with particular attention on developing a battery for locomotive use. Three different calls went out for participants during the course of the contest, which did manage to produce some solid technological results. But in the end, it fell short of achieving the kind of "electrical storage device" that Toyoda had envisioned.

Work continued, however, at the research lab until Japan's defeat in World War II. But Toyoda's vision continued to inspire inventors and innovators, and instilled a nationwide recognition of the importance of R&D. "Remain at the vanguard of the times through endless creativity, inquisitiveness and pursuit of improvement," was one of Toyoda's lasting mottos, which eventually became one of Toyota's five core principles.

The Toyota Motor Company was founded in 1937 by Sakichi Toyoda's son, Kiichiro, after spending some time as a division within Toyota Industries. In late 1939, Toyota parted ways with the Imperial Institute of Invention and Innovation to set up its own research facility in "power storage devices" for automobiles. But this time, there was greater urgency to the task than just winning a contest. As Japan geared up for war, gasoline became increasingly scarce. The development of alternative energy along with the electric automobile suddenly assumed immense importance.

After Germany invaded Poland, setting off World War II, the flow of academic and technological exchanges between Japan and the West dried up, leaving Japanese researchers on their own. Toyota sought to pool its resources by bringing all the technical talent it could muster under one roof. The Toyota Physical & Chemical Research Institute was born, dedicated to applied physical and chemical research for industrial purposes. Headed by Kiichiro Toyoda as executive director, and his elder brother-in-law, Risaburo, as director, the board was packed with dozens of professors from the country's leading universities, including Tokyo Imperial University and Tohoku Imperial University.

Once again, the effort failed to produce the desired results. But again, it did succeed in laying the structural and disciplinary foundation for research in both vehicle and electrical battery development that would one day find its way to the hybrid car.

On my annual visits to the Detroit Auto Show, I always make it a point to visit the Henry Ford Museum, just outside Detroit in Dearborn, Michigan, to brush up on my automotive history. There, on display, is an early electric vehicle. Each time I see it, I'm reminded of Sakichi Toyoda, and wonder whether he would've been more surprised to find out that his challenge was so universally shared, or by the fact that, to this day, it has not yet been answered.

The Prius is Born

Toyota's efforts in what we might call the "alternative" or "green" technologies realm resumed gradually after World War II. Beginning in the latter half of the 1960s, Toyota engineers got to work developing the gas turbine engine, the rotary engine, and the electric car in addition to the reciprocating, or piston, engine. Amid their pursuit for many different systems, they subjected their engines to painstakingly detailed review and refinement down to every last component. That was the way things were done at Toyota, and it constituted progress. But there were two milestone events that really drove Toyota, and every automaker, to new heights in their developmental drive. One was the 1973 oil crisis when the Organization of Petroleum Exporting Countries (OPEC) placed an embargo on oil shipments to the west, including Japan, for supporting Israel in the Yom Kippur War. And the other was the *Clean Air Act 1970* (often referred to as the Muskie Act), which for the first time set stringent limits on automobile-engine emissions in the U.S.

Although enforcement of the Clean Air Act was eventually postponed, the Japanese government followed suit in 1975 with its own "Japanese Muskie Act," enforcing tailpipe-emission regulations in Japan that would become the most rigorous in the world.

From a technological standpoint, emission controls had placed the automotive industry in wholly uncharted territory, because none of the technology it possessed to date could really be effectively applied. In particular, the simultaneous reduction of carbon monoxide (CO), hydrocarbons (HC), and nitrogen oxides (NO_x) posed extreme technical challenges because of their inverse relationship with each other: less of one would produce more of the other.

After an arduous period of trial and error, Toyota succeeded in arriving at a satisfying balance of emissions controls, fuel efficiency, and cost performance, gradually shedding its image as relatively passive toward environmental issues.

Another critical event that awakened Toyota to the importance of green technology for its survival came when Toyota faced a performance crisis in 1993. Toyota's pretax profits for 1993 dipped to their lowest levels since 1982, when the Toyota Motor Company merged with the Toyota Motor Sales Company to form today's Toyota.

In Japan's general election that year, the ruling Liberal Democratic Party (LDP) had lost its majority in the Diet, and subsequently its hold on power for the first time since the end of the war. In August, a coalition government composed of eight parties under opposition leader Morihiro Hosokawa took charge. Paralleling the volatility of the political realm was an extremely rapid appreciation of the yen, a situation that was aggravated by sluggish auto sales at home.

"If we break below 100 yen to the dollar, even momentarily, it will become extremely difficult to secure any profits at all," lamented a Toyota executive at the annual earnings announcement, who seemed horrified at the thought that Toyota might slip into the red ink.

It was also about this time that Shoichiro Toyoda, who had assumed chairmanship of the company the previous year after serving as its president for a decade, drew attention for grumbling, "Toyota cars are boring. They all look the same."

The G21 Project

It was amid this sense of crisis that R&D executive vice president Yoshiro Kimbara called together his engineers and commanded them to discard all their preconceived notions about car design to date, and with a clean slate begin thinking long and hard about building an automobile for the twenty-first century. In September 1993, Kimbara launched a research committee dubbed the "G21 Project," "G" standing for "generation" and "21" for the coming century. It was to be "zero base" research, meaning that its members would be discouraged from looking to the past for cues, so as not to be shackled by it. They were going to create and then set the standard for what a mass-market sedan in the coming century should look like.

Toyota president Toyoda immediately jumped aboard. "Get it done," he said. So did former chairman Eiji Toyoda, who had overseen the production of Toyota's original standard-setting car for the masses, the flagship Corolla.

If Sakichi Toyoda was the "father of the Toyota Group", and Kiichiro the "father of Toyota Motor Company," then Eiji Toyoda, Kiichiro's first cousin, would be the "father of modern Toyota." Eiji had spearheaded Toyota's "restoration," expanded the company overseas and planted roots in U.S. soil. And now as honorary executive chairman, with no voting power, the G21 idea had him excited again. "If only I were a little bit younger, this is a project I'd like to handle," the octogenarian beamed.

Eiji Toyoda had also been quick to predict the rapid change in current that accompanied the bursting of the bubble economy in the early 1990s in Japan, and had repeatedly expressed his gut feeling that Toyota needed a whole new way of thinking about building cars.

The G21 Project set sail with only a vague idea of what it wanted to accomplish: to build a compact sedan that was "extremely fuel efficient" and "environmentally friendly." By the end of the year, however, this fuzzy notion had some twenty handpicked managers and engineers working on it.

Team leader and chief engineer for the project was Takeshi Uchiyamada, an experienced Toyota veteran, who was still young enough to embrace change wholeheartedly. A baby-boomer born in 1946, Uchiyamada had also proven himself a capable manager, having just streamlined Toyota's entire technical division, the largest such reform in its history. But Uchiyamada's love was research. Ever since entering the company in 1969, he had spent most of his time devising ways to reduce engine vibration and noise. Uchiyamada got quickly to work selecting a team of about ten junior engineers in their early thirties to cover the whole spectrum of automotive development, from body and chassis to engine, power train, and even manufacturing methods.

As soon as the G21 staff were formally announced in February 1994, Uchiyamada gathered his team together, and laid out the ground rules. "Our first priority is to set up the right kind of work environment. That means basing everything out of one room so information is effectively shared. We need a system that really concentrates our efforts on building the twenty-first-century car. Second, each member of the project must set his aspirations high if we are to succeed in developing a truly groundbreaking vehicle."

The first thing the project produced was a plethora of slogans, dubbed the "G21 Code of Conduct," to guide the group's activities: emphasize speed, publish and disseminate conference minutes immediately, don't postpone decisions, share information, don't criticize, but suggest, and place the project's interests over the individual interests of one's department or division.

The sense of urgency was fueled by a companywide fear that a crisis was looming on the horizon for Toyota if changes weren't made. With the G21 Project came the quiet hope that Toyota, fueled by a sense of crisis, might become galvanized around an ambitious challenge, and, ultimately, find its true bearings for the next century.

Traditionally at Toyota, once the decision to launch a new model is made, a chief engineer (CE) is named to take charge of the entire development process, from planning and development all the way to product rollout. Formerly called a *shusa* (project manager), it is a job entrusted with immense responsibility. Although the G21 Project was not under any pressure to develop a specific vehicle in the conventional sense, Uchiyama interpreted his role to be similar to that of a CE, and carried out his duties in accordance with that understanding.

In the case of the first generation Crown, Corolla, or any other new model conceived and developed at Toyota, there had always been one person serving as kind of a permanent project manager, the "senior *shusa*." That person was senior managing director Tatsuo Hasegawa. He had laid out all the rules and guidelines pertaining to the CE in the form of ten written articles. They included such mandates as "always endeavor to develop a wide range of knowledge and insight," and "have your own policy and strategy for getting things done." Uchiyamada based his G21 Project code of conduct on Hasegawa's philosophy.

For the next five months, the G21 Project team met regularly, conducting a variety of studies and tests aimed at establishing the concept for a compact car deserving of the twenty-first-century moniker; one that would be "low on environmental impact and high on efficiency." And then in July, it compiled its results for review and assessment by management, and disbanded. Specifically, what it came up with was an ambitious plan to build a vehicle with a compact body but a long wheelbase, a high roof, a spacious cabin, and a highly-efficient 1.5-liter, direct-injection, four-cylinder engine.

The proposal was instantly lambasted as having set its sights far too low. Here was a product that was supposed to represent

Toyota's answer to the demands of the twenty-first century, and all it strived to achieve was a meager 1.5-fold increase in fuel efficiency.

Enter the Hybrid Engine

As fortune would have it, there was another project taking place concurrently in the electric vehicle (EV) development unit. It was a project to develop a hybrid engine system. EV development had been under way as far back as 1971, as part of a transportation ministry initiative designed to respond to the strict emissions regulations being enacted at home and abroad. Toyota actually started delivering operational EVs based on the Toyota Town Ace to various government agencies in Japan, and work had begun to provide an EV-drive system for Toyota's luxury sedan, the Crown Majesta. In the process, EV engineers at Toyota had begun looking into hybrid systems that used a combination of two power sources: electric motor and gasoline engine.

The man heading up hybrid system prototype development in the EV unit was Masanao Shiomi, who had already tasted success as CE for the best-selling Toyota van, the Town Ace. Shiomi had been intrigued by electric motors due to the overwhelmingly low levels of heat, noise, and vibration they produced in comparison to gasoline engines. Shiomi rolled up his sleeves and eagerly began converting the Town Ace and Crown Majesta into EV prototypes. But he soon found himself butting up against fundamental issues such as how to secure an acceptable driving distance with an EV when there is no battery-recharging infrastructure in place. Shiomi came to the conclusion that to make the EV commercially viable, he would either have to improve the battery radically—which we know from Sakichi Toyoda's challenge was a formidable feat—or figure out some method for securing a continuous supply of electricity to the motor within the vehicle. Shiomi chose the latter, and within days found himself in the office of executive vice president Akihiro Wada, passionately extolling how the EV issue could be overcome through a hybrid system capable of running continuously by marrying an electric motor to a gasoline engine that, in its operation, could recharge the battery.

This, of course, was nothing new. The hybrid EV already had a long history. An American engineer named H. Piper had filed for a patent in 1905 for his design of a hybrid vehicle with an electric motor that augmented power. Piper believed that the combination of electric and gasoline motors would help the vehicle accelerate to a robust 25 miles per hour in ten seconds, as opposed to the thirty seconds it took with a gasoline engine alone. Three-and-a-half years later, Piper was issued the patent.

Some hybrid cars were invented around this time with similar objectives in mind, including the first commercial production of a hybrid car in France in 1909. But over time, gasoline engines improved in power, and were made even more convenient when the electric self-starter replaced the hand crank. Experimentation with hybrid technology continued for a while, only to die out around 1920.

It wasn't until the 1970s that there was renewed interest in hybrid and electric car development in the U.S., again, in the wake of the oil shocks and an antipollution movement. Automakers came out with alternative propulsion prototypes, including a parallel hybrid taxi by VW, and a parallel hybrid truck by Japanese automaker Daihatsu. But once gasoline became plentiful again, the hybrid fervor quickly dissipated.

Fast forward about twenty years to the 1990s, and we find a second wave of hybrid-car development prompted by a resurgence in global concern about environmental degradation, the depletion of natural resources from the world's oil reserves to forests and fisheries, and the need to re-examine economic development across the world so that it could come at less of a cost to the natural environment. An increase in the magnitude of natural disasters, aberrational climate patterns, and ozone-layer depletion also fueled a growing consensus that mankind was overtaxing its natural habitat to an extent that could no longer be ignored.

So once again, auto companies began refocusing more of their research budgets on the kinds of alternative technologies they had grown accustomed to shelving. In Europe, French automaker Peugeot produced a series of hybrid prototype cars based on its front-wheel-drive platform, while Swedish Volvo grappled with a gas turbine-powered hybrid.

In the U.S., President Bill Clinton in 1993 launched his Partnership for a New Generation of Vehicles (PNGV) consortium, a cooperative research program between the U.S. government and major auto corporations, aimed at establishing U.S. leadership in the development of affordable, extremely fuel-efficient, and low-emission vehicles that could meet driver needs. The PNGV challenge was: "Build a car with up to 80 miles per gallon at the level of performance, utility, and cost of ownership that today's consumers demand."

Hybrids offered the most immediate solution, particularly diesel-electric hybrid technology. GM, Ford, and DaimlerChrysler had already been hard at work in this area. But diesel engines were subject to stringent emissions standards in the U.S., not to mention a bad public image, due to the noise and black smoke they belched out. And regular gasoline continued to offer comparatively better price stability. Diesel hybrid development in the 1990s eventually got placed on the back burner.

GM did succeed, however, in leapfrogging the hybrid process with a public release of an EV called the EV1, which produced no emissions and got 60 miles to the gallon. Partly funded by Clinton's PNGV, its development had been largely prompted by a mandate issued by the state of California, which had grown increasingly concerned about deteriorating air quality. California wanted auto companies to make 10 percent of all new cars sold in the state meet zero-emission standards by 2003. The EV was only produced for a couple of years between 1997 and 1999, and was available only through limited lease without an option to buy. Toyota, Honda, and Ford also came out with their own EVs, in a variety of form factors ranging from SUVs to pickup trucks. But while these vehicles proved popular among the environmentally conscious, first adopters, and well-heeled celebrities who could afford the steep monthly payments, automakers eventually pulled the plug on their EV programs, citing lack of immediate profitability and practicality.

Toyota Targets Tokyo Motor Show 1995 for Hybrid Debut

Engineers, including Shiomi in the Toyota EV division in Japan, were encouraged by what they felt was a gathering momentum of support for their work. Here was an opportunity to take advantage of the know-how they had accumulated in EVs, and apply it to the development of a hybrid power train that could be unique to Toyota.

The basic plan was to rely on an electric motor at startup, when the burden on the engine is greatest, and then switch to the gasoline engine at speeds beyond 28 miles per hour when a gas engine can run most efficiently. A sophisticated onboard computer system would be able to calculate precisely when each power source should be used, and essentially toggle between them. At times when running the gas engine would be inefficient, such as when parked or stuck in traffic, it would be automatically switched off. The energy generated when running the engine could also be used to recharge the battery. The vehicle would therefore be highly fuel efficient, and emit considerably fewer emissions, making it perfectly worthy of being dubbed "the car for the twenty-first century." The G21's initial goal of a 1.5-fold increase suddenly paled in comparison with the technological potential that had just been presented to them, and from this moment, the talk turned to, "Okay, how much more mileage can we get?"

"Here's our chance to let the world know that Toyota is working toward a next-generation automobile that will get superior fuel economy and be easy on the environment," Shiomi excitedly told Wada, who then gave his consent to build the compact G21 economy car on a hybrid system.

In November 1994, when Uchiyamada paid a visit to Wada's office to give him a briefing on the G21 project, Wada waited until Uchiyamada was finished before quietly responding with, "Why don't we take your project, and present it as a hybrid concept at next year's Tokyo Motor Show?" Uchiyamada's mouth dropped. He had no issue with the notion of making a hybrid car as a show model, but it was still in early development and not anywhere close to being considered for the market.

But Toyota management had already made up its mind. It was looking to be first in something for a change, and that would be the hybrid. "I don't want simply an extension of past technology. I don't want to build just another economy car. We have to rethink development, and if that means building a hybrid car that gets twice the fuel efficiency of any other car out there and exhibiting it at the Motor Show, that's what we'll do." Eventually, Uchiyamada concurred.

As soon as the sun rose on 1995, a brand new team was launched to find the most practical, fuel-efficient hybrid system for the G21. Dubbed "BRVF Phase I," "BR" stood for "business reform" and referred to short-term projects the technical administration division had set up to tackle problem areas that individual departments couldn't solve on their own. "VF" stood for "vehicle fuel economy."

The team consisted of four members, headed by Yuichi Fujii, president of the Panasonic EV Energy Company, a nickel-metal hydride (NiMH) battery manufacturer jointly owned by the Matsushita Group and Toyota. The first order of business was to hit the books, essentially, and examine the dozen or so different types of hybrid systems that were already in existence, either in theory or practice.

Series Versus Parallel

Hybrid cars combining engine and electric motor have been proposed in different configurations. But there hasn't really been one solution that stands head and shoulders above the rest. The BRVF team had to evaluate each type of hybrid application, and narrow them down to those that had the potential for doubling fuel efficiency, which was the team's primary goal.

As a quick overview, there are two types of hybrid systems: "series" and "parallel." In a series hybrid, the engine provides primary energy to a generator that converts the energy to electricity so it can run the motor, which in turn provides power to the transmission. The electricity that is generated gets stored in batteries for long-term use. Because the flow of energy is a series of steps, it is called a "series hybrid." In a "parallel" hybrid, both the electric motor and the combustion engine work in tandem, or in parallel, to power the transmission in a complementary fashion. At low speeds or low power output, engine efficiency is poor, so the motor takes charge of the vehicle. At higher speeds, such as in freeway driving, the engine is most efficient, so the two power sources work interchangeably or in combination to achieve the highest energy efficiency depending on driving conditions.

With the 1995 Tokyo Motor Show fast approaching, the BRVF team didn't have much time. The primary research would have to be completed in about three months. So while it continued with its studies, it came to the conclusion that it could get a hybrid system with the maximum fuel efficiency by fusing the series and parallel hybrid models together. In short, it wanted a system that would use the gasoline engine only when absolutely necessary, and so save on fuel consumption.

In May, Fujii presented the team's findings to executive vice president Wada. Wada gave his immediate blessing and told them to go build a prototype. In June, Toyota's executive technical advisory committee had signed off on the plan to commoditize a hybrid system, and install it in the high fuel-efficiency compact car that the G21 team had proposed. At this point, everyone outside top management believed that the aim was to announce Toyota's first hybrid car in April 1998. That was still three years away.

One major challenge the team faced right out of the blocks was that Toyota did not manufacture the primary components needed for a hybrid system. The hybrid nucleus of battery, motor, and inverter to control the motor were all electrical, not mechanical, products, a realm quite alien from an engine-centric automaker.

One of the principal drawbacks to a series hybrid system is that electricity has to be generated twice, once when the engine is powering the generator, and again to run the motor from the generator. While it's an effective system at low speeds, the exact reverse is true at high speeds. The parallel hybrid system, by contrast, can alternately provide required power either from the motor or engine. But the engine remains on at all times, which doesn't produce great fuel savings.

The BRVF group decided to first focus its attention on the gasoline engine's poor efficiency at low speeds, because only about

20 percent of its energy is actually used. The natural conclusion was to dispense with using the gasoline engine at startup, or at any other time when it couldn't be operating in its most efficient state. It also decided to take advantage of a unique characteristic of the electric motor called "regenerative braking." This is a method for harnessing the heat energy released during braking, and converting it to electricity to recharge the battery, basically pinch-hitting for the engine in that task. This would help limit the use of the gasoline engine only to instances when it was absolutely necessary or most efficient to do so. The rest of the time, the vehicle would be powered by battery. This would surely produce significant fuel-efficiency gains.

On paper, the team figured it could squeeze as much as 28 kilometers per liter of gas (66 miles per gallon) out of a Camry-class car with a 1.5-liter engine. That, quite providentially, was "double" the current performance of its standard gas-powered version. The group had its "Toyota Hybrid System (THS)."

Splitting Headache

The moment the green light was given to develop the THS, phase two of the BRVF was launched. An important addition to the group was senior staff engineer Takehisa Yaegashi, the man who would one day be considered by many as the "father" of the first-generation Prius.

Joining Toyota back in 1969, Yaegashi was a veteran of comprehensive engine systems design, and Toyota's top emissions man. When EV development returned to the front burner around 1989 in response to California's zero-emissions mandate, Yaegashi traveled to the U.S., together with technical senior manager, Shinichi Kato, to gain some insight into EV development. He returned from the trip convinced that an EV alone could not satisfy people's automotive needs, but that a hybrid could. Both depth and breadth were added to the team with Engineering Division I staff leader Hideaki Matsui in charge of the drive train, and Future Project Division I manager Shoichi Sasaki taking over electrical systems.

The work of the second BRVF group began with the power-source development team trying to figure out how to fit a hybrid system into the G21 project's compact specs. The body-design team essentially had to start from scratch to re-examine a body, chassis, and overall layout that could accommodate any hybrid system at all. The physical challenges sparked constant debate over precisely what kind of hybrid system it could, or wanted to, exhibit at the Motor Show.

The issue was essentially debated between those who favored just the idea of incredible fuel efficiency, and those who felt it necessary to integrate features that would expand the G21 concept further, such as improvements in riding comfort. Eventually, the team concluded that jaw-dropping fuel-efficiency figures would be enough for a motor-show model. In addition, it settled on a hybrid system featuring a direct fuel injection engine and the latest continuously variable transmission (CVT), currently the most efficient way to run a gasoline engine.

But now came the hard part: designing it. The group's members quickly realized that their summer vacations would be lost as they anguished over how to divide the workload between the motor and the engine, and subsequently how to build the control system accordingly. How much driving power would they want at a certain speed? How many kilowatts of power should the engine provide? How much should the motor provide? They needed to decide upon an algorithm for onboard computers to control the different power allocation variables systematically and automatically, and get the engine and motor to respond accordingly.

Technically, they had the answer in a power-split device called a "planetary gear set," which can distribute power seamlessly between the gas and electric-drive motor, and let the car run as either a parallel hybrid or series hybrid. The control of this ingeniously conceived means for splitting or combining engine and motor power, however, would fall hard on the system's multiple onboard computers. The problem was that the computer software they had was not only unreliable, it often failed to run at all. "I didn't come to Toyota to work on computers; I came to work on cars," Uchiyamada was heard to say.

The Prius Stalls

When the curtain opened on the Thirty-first Tokyo Motor Show on October 27, 1995, Toyota unveiled its very first hybrid concept car: the "Prius," taken from the Latin word meaning "to go before." It was a name that perfectly suited the G21 Project's pursuit of something new that was not tethered to precedent. As planned, fuel efficiency was its main attraction, boasting 30 kilometers to the liter (70.56 miles per gallon)! That was a simulated figure though. Its rechargeable battery, which powered the electric motor, was still under development by the Matsushita Battery Industrial Co..

The first battery for the Prius had less than half the capability that Toyota was hoping for, and at twice the desired size, proved completely impractical. Ultimately, an appropriate battery would not be ready in time for the show, so the Prius on display housed, quite ridiculously, an electric condenser.

But the "30 kilometers per liter" claim was more than enough to generate tremendous buzz. Senior technical manager Shinichi Kato found himself fielding a barrage of questions from domestic and foreign media about this mileage-busting prototype. Although the Prius at this stage was little more than a next-generation "econo-car," that Toyota had pre-empted its competition and come this far with a hybrid technology caused enough of a commotion, which in turn strengthened the resolve inside Toyota toward a commercial release. The Prius would be Toyota's first mass-production hybrid car. The only people not celebrating were the project's engineers, who still had a daunting list of obstacles to overcome.

November saw the commemorative road test of the first-generation Prius, and the first instance of the car's complete failure to move. A software glitch. One of the biggest promises of the Prius was its ability to run solely on electric motor, gas engine, or a combination of both, and to be able to switch automatically among the three methods as necessary without the driver ever noticing. The computer software determined when and to what degree this switching should take place. It had to figure out and select the appropriate propulsion method for optimizing power and efficiency. But that also meant that even the slightest computer bug could bring the whole process to a screeching halt. The Prius was, at heart, computer technology, and it bore a heavy risk for it. The team also found at the test run that it couldn't turn on the engine without a whole lot of shaking going on.

But these setbacks weren't about to dampen the mood among president Hiroshi Okuda and top management for faster development of the Prius. Uchiyamada, too, viewed rapid development of his prototype as a chance to take a very symbolic lead in the auto industry, and rejuvenate the company's image. So he called on each design team to work harder.

By the following February, the often inert Prius was running. Cries of jubilation rose up over the test course. But again, after cruising along happily for 500 yards, the Prius just stopped. This couldn't be an issue of not having the technology. Simulations repeatedly showed that it all worked.

Then the Toyota board of directors dropped a bombshell. They wanted the Prius to go into production a year earlier than originally planned, at the end of 1997, and asked Uchiyamada to lay out a concrete schedule.

Hiroshi Okuda Applies the Pressure

Illness had forced previous president Tatsuro Toyoda to step down in August 1995 in the middle of his term, and make way for Hiroshi Okuda. Okuda was stepping into the presidency as the first non-Toyoda family member to head the company since Toyota Motor Company had merged with Toyota Motor Sales Company in 1982. Okuda took over hoping to flush out the stagnant air that had permeated the company by essentially speeding things up and blazing a trail of innovation. He had been enthusiastic about the hybrid car from the start, and wanted it out as soon as possible.

When Okuda formally assumed the presidency on August 25, 1995, he summoned his leaders from all departments and made clear his intent to instill a mood of crisis.

We're at a critical junction in this industry; and how we respond in the next year or two will surely augur whether we continue to grow in the next century, or become a relic of the past century. Maintaining the status quo would be disastrous for Toyota. We have to move boldly, quickly, and not shrink from the trial-and-error process. We need to reassess how we invest our management resources, and better empower the great young talent we have so they can try new things freely.

By April of 1996, Okuda had laid forth a revised "Toyota Environmental Action Plan," listing 20 specifically articulated items and objectives including reducing emissions and developing clean-energy vehicles.

The Toyota that Okuda had inherited was indeed facing a management crisis. It was losing ground to rival makers in overseas expansion, and its domestic share of the auto market had dropped below 40 percent. Toyota was beginning to show classic symptoms of "large company disease": too much process and not enough action, overspecialization, and poor communication. Okuda was determined to restore an aggressiveness or frontier spirit to the culture and climate. The Prius was the perfect vehicle for selling the concept of a forward-thinking, green Toyota that could lead the world into the next century.

A shudder of panic, however, spread through the Prius team under the new imperative. Battery performance was only half what was needed. There wasn't even any indication that the inverter-control software that would be needed to regulate the flow of electricity to the motor would be developed in time. Plus the procurement cost of the parts needed for production was simply too high. Requisite components, including the battery, motor, and inverter, were still too large to squeeze into the narrow dimensions of a passenger car.

Uchiyamada found himself pleading with Wada. "We're more than willing to work as hard as humanly possible, but if a technical impossibility arises, postponing the release must remain an option for us."

Okuda knew that he was asking a lot, and was willing to throw whatever resources the company could muster at the project. He actively made sure that the project had an ample budget to work with, as well as extra personnel waiting in the wings. At the time, there were more than twenty high-priority projects under way. But in what was an extraordinary measure, Okuda decided to shift 60 percent of the company's developmental strength to hybrid-car development. And he cleared a hybrid prototype production line to be available twenty-four hours a day, seven days a week.

When 1996 came along, Uchiyamada felt his confidence returning. He did away with the old "G21" label that symbolized the planning stage era, and retagged it with the project development code name, "890T."

When a project is put on a product-planning schedule, Toyota has the practice of attaching the letter "Z" to it. In order to distinguish it from other "Z" projects, another letter is added, as in the case of the Crown, "ZS." The Prius team added a small case "i" to the "Z," standing for "intelligence," and more symbolically, earning it the distinction of a full-on, product development program.

Takeshi Uchiyamada officially became one of four chief engineers for the newly christened Zi Project. As part of the development program that comes with the "Z" label, he was joined by executive product-planning engineers Shunji Ishida, Satoshi Ogiso, and Toshiyuki Oi. Together, they established a product-planning office. Ogiso was put in charge of hybrid system and chassis, Ishida covered body interior and exterior design, and Oi was to oversee the progress of the project overall.

Uchiyamada affectionately compared the Prius project with NASA's 1960 Apollo space exploration program, likening it to the heroic mobilization of U.S. technological and scientific talent after the successful 1957 mission of the first artificial satellite, *Sputnik*, by the Soviet Union. It would eventually result in NASA successfully landing a man on the Moon, and bringing him safely home. Uchiyamada was finding inspiration where he could.

The technology was within reach, but like the Apollo program in its early stages, it was still a complete unknown whether they could really "get to the Moon." For the Prius project, no one had painted a clear masterplan until now. But gradually, as the elemental technologies for the hybrid began to fall into place, the project began to take on the aspect of a blueprint for Toyota's future.

Fighter Jet *Shusui*

Right about this time, Uchiyamada came across a log documenting the development of the advanced experimental, rocket-powered fighter aircraft, *Shusui*, or Mitsubishi J8M, which the Japanese military hurried to develop in the closing months of World War II to intercept and destroy American bombers. In July 1944, engineers from various divisions of the imperial Japanese navy, air force, and army assembled at the Yokosuka Navy Yard with private-sector representatives from the Nakajima Aircraft Co., Mitsubishi Aircraft Co., Ishikawajima Heavy Industries Co., Hitachi Ltd., and Tokyo Shibaura Electric Co. ("Toshiba"), to open a research committee. They decided to develop a rocket-powered fighter aircraft for use by both the army and navy. The interceptor *Shusui* (a.k.a. Ki-100) would be conceived as a means for reversing the tide of the war. The navy would lead fuselage development, the army would handle fuel and chemicals, and production would go to Mitsubishi Aircraft, well known as the manufacturer of the "Zero" fighter.

Construction of the *Shusui* took six months longer than planned. But in June 1945, it was finished, and five planes were actually produced by the end of the war. It ultimately didn't prove to be the tide-turning miracle weapon that was hoped for, but that Japanese engineers had taken a completely unknown realm of rocket development and within the space of a year made it a reality emboldened Uchiyamada greatly.

"You can achieve the impossible when you really have to," he commented. And every time some new progress was made in the elemental technology for the Prius, Uchiyamada would load up a prototype, and try it again. A new prototype was built at a rate of once every two or three months, as he conveyed to team members his determination to finish in time.

The project also began to change the way cars were built at Toyota. Every division had what was called "the ant army," where hundreds of hands would descend on a product once in full developmental swing. But here, it was decided that a new operational method, "Simultaneous Engineering" (SE), was to be implemented, so that designers, draftspeople, and production engineers could work together more effectively and efficiently, enabling information to be shared and know-how to be spread throughout all the teams involved. It was a brand new management style at the time, quickly forming the backbone of the group's modus operandi.

The launch of the Zi team was accompanied by fully fledged commencement of tests of the THS. But since the Prius THS was a system built on continuously switching the engine on and off, a method had to be devised to achieve this as smoothly as possible. So far, however, the car remained rife with problems: slow acceleration, short battery life, noise, and vibration. What's more, nobody had decided on a design for the car, even as plans for a release date were being etched into stone.

"Let's have a design contest. On a grand scale!" Uchiyamada exclaimed at a meeting of the newly inaugurated Prius product-planning office. A total of nine teams took part, including those from Toyota design offices in the U.S. and Europe. It was the first large-scale design contest that Toyota had ever held. After all was said and done, one design truly stood out for sporting the kind of fresh, innovative, and futuristic look a car for the next century ought to have. It was the entry of a designer named Irwin Lui at Toyota's Calty design studio in Newport Beach, California.

As preparations were being made for bringing the Prius to market, in March 1996, the third phase of the BRVF group was formed, led by Takehisa Yaegashi. Hideaki Matsui would continue to lead power train development, with Shinichi Abe in charge of engine, and Shoichi Sasaki team leader of electrical systems.

Abe grappled with how to overcome the vibration every time the engine started up. A piston is compressed as it moves up in the cylinder, meeting with tremendous force. But once past the compression point, it eases up, creating vibration. Fortunately, Toyota had an in-house solution already available in its Variable Valve Timing with Intelligence (VVT-i) technology. It could variably alter the optimal opening and closing timing of the air-intake valve from low to high revolution, thus suppressing vibration when the engine is turned on and off.

Another problem that loomed as large as the engine on-off challenge was the electronics. In 1991, when momentum gathered for

EV as the only automotive solution capable of meeting zero-emissions standards, Toyota was prompted to establish an EV research division inside its electronics division. In 1992, Masanao Shiomi amalgamated all the EV research that was going on inside the company, and created an EV research division within the Vehicle Development Center III, which he then directed.

In 1995, Toyota released an EV called the RAV4 EV, powered by a rechargeable NiMH battery. When EV development began, Toyota had to make do with electric motors brought in from outside the company. But the more electric power-train development proceeded, the more basic components not manufactured inside Toyota would become a necessity. So the automaker began manufacturing the motor and parts itself. The electric drive components for the Prius primarily made use of EV technology developed for the RAV4 EV.

But where an EV would be powered solely on the strength of its onboard battery, the hybrid system would derive its power from an electric motor and gas engine. This required a unified system for controlling and synchronizing the engine, the motor, and the generator. Moreover, something was needed to skillfully act as a power split device capable of controlling power from these three sources (engine, electric motor, and generator) depending on driving circumstances. This important role fell to the aforementioned planetary gear. The Prius also needed a battery that was much smaller than that used in the RAV4.

Knocking Down Challenges, One at a Time

Yaegashi knew he had to establish reliable control of such a complicated nexus of technologies. So he began building a simulation system capable of better pinpointing the various junctures where problems arose in a running prototype. As a result, he was able to confirm what was going wrong; where the flaws in the communication system lay; when the hybrid system's computer wasn't effectively transmitting commands regarding how much power the battery needed; and when the motor was not supplying power. Thus he was able to expose the reasons the prototype Prius often failed to move.

In addition to a computer that can oversee the operation of the hybrid system as a whole, specific computers are needed to control the engine, electricity generation, and brakes, monitor battery performance, and even control other computers, such as those that tell the driver what is going on in the car, particularly when something isn't working properly. In a mass-production vehicle, performance has to be guaranteed. It has to work all the time, and bringing it up to that level was an immense challenge.

Building a practical battery posed an even more formidable test. With the van-type RAV4, there was room under the floor to lay down a gigantic battery. But what is required with a passenger sedan is a small, lightweight, yet high-performance battery that can fit, say, upright in the space between the rear seats and the trunk.

The battery consisted of 240 inline, 1.2-volt NiMH "cells" boxed together as one battery, which, as one can imagine, took up considerable space. The team succeeded, however, in reducing what had been two sets of batteries to one, while still securing high performance.

NiMH batteries tend to exhibit sudden drops in performance after extended use. So the team developed a control system for measuring and adjusting the amount of charge, so that the battery would never be charged or undercharged beyond what was required.

The inverter, which controls electricity to the motor, is an extremely heat-sensitive device. In EVs that have no gas engine, one can install the battery, inverter, and motor together under the floor of the vehicle, and let the natural circulation of air cool the system. The Prius motor is placed next to the gasoline engine, with all the heat, vibration, and noise it generates, so it needs its own dedicated cooling device. The team decided to run water underneath not only the generator and motor, but also below the inverter as a coolant.

In June 1996, two technical managers newly promoted to directors, Hiroyuki Watanabe and Kazuo Okamoto, were added to the list of officers in charge of Prius development, in what amounted to Uchiyamada's project being elevated to a companywide project in form, if not yet in substance. But this meant an even clearer distinction of roles. Matsushita was to build the battery cells, while the Toyota group would build the modules and holders to link them. Toyota and Matsushita would then jointly assemble the batteries at a newly created company called Panasonic EV Energy. Toyota was now deeply involved in building a future on electrical and computer technology, and there would be no turning back.

Another Shocker

No sooner had the Prius team settled into its new roles than it was hit with another bombshell announcement. At the March 1997 Toyota board meeting, the date for completing the hybrid system was moved up, and a release date announced for the end of the year! Granted, many technical problems had been solved, and the Prius was mobile, but confidence in reaching its fuel-efficiency marks by launch date was still low. And then came the press announcement.

"A Toyota hybrid sedan with double the fuel economy and one-tenth the emissions of a regular gasoline car projected for release in November." That was the headline in Japan's leading business daily, the *Nihon Keizai Shimbun*, on March 26, 1997, complete with a description of the THS and a conversation with executive vice president Wada.

The details were left out, but the article did say that the car would have a 1.5-liter engine with maximum speed in excess of 100 kilometers per hour (62 miles per hour), and retail about only $5,000 over the price of a conventional gasoline model. What was made numerically clear, however, was the doubled mileage it would get, at 28 kilometers per liter (65.86 miles per gallon), and the November target for its release. Any avenue of retreat for the engineers had now been cut off.

Takehisa Yaegashi reflected on how he felt afterwards. "It felt like jumping into the deep end of a pool. But at the same time, I knew this would launch Toyota as the first automaker in the world with a true twenty-first-century production car, so we were ready to see it through."

Actually, there was a renewed sense of exuberance in the announcement. When the last round of clean-car competition had taken place in the early 1970s, Honda had dealt the first blow, selling cars with its Compound Vortex Controlled Combustion (CVCC) device for reducing auto emissions. Toyota, on the other hand, had not been reading the tealeaves. The company had a wealth of car models and engines, but was slow in responding to the cleaner emissions current, and its engineers drew a barrage of criticism for their inability to meet the demands of the Muskie Act.

This time, however, "Toyota would lead the way with hybrid-car development," remarked Yaegashi. With the March press announcement providing a renewed impetus, the development team turned to around-the-clock testing of the Prius. During its peak in the summer of 1997, they took it out for repeated spins up and down the famously narrow and serpentine Wada Pass in the mountains outside Tokyo, checking for power dropoffs, gauging the effects of repeated engine use and disuse, and driving for three hours with the airconditioner on at full blast.

A Spectacular Debut

Having finished testing by the end of August 1997, the Prius quietly went into prototype production on an assembly line in the corner of the Takaoka factory, where Corollas are made. Toyota was producing most of the components, including the motor, the inverter, and the rectifying converter, in house for the first time—except for the battery, which Toyota and Matsushita were jointly manufacturing.

Two months later, in October, the world's first production hybrid passenger car was unveiled to the media inside the Phoenix Hall at the ANA Hotel in Tokyo's upscale Roppongi district. President Okuda's mood was one of exaltation: "This Prius was born from a challenge to reform Toyota. It is a proposal of new values for the automobile in the twenty-first century."

Both Okuda and executive vice president Wada boarded the Prius, and with Uchiyamada behind the wheel, drove it along the thick plush carpet of the conference area and into the next room. There was no exhaust, and almost no noise. A month later in November, the Prius would be named Japan's Car of the Year.

In December, the Third Session of the Conference of the Parties to the United Nations Framework Convention on Climate Change was held in Kyoto, resulting in the Kyoto Protocol, which set binding targets on Europe, the U.S., Japan, and the nations of the world to reduce their CO_2 emissions. That same month, production of the Prius for sales in the domestic market went online at the Takaoka assembly plant outside Nagoya. The tape-cutting ceremony was presided over not only by Toyota chairman Shoichiro Toyoda and President Okuda, but also the head of the labor union. In dramatic fashion, the Prius was born.

In the time between its announcement and release, some 2,000 orders had been placed, significantly exceeding the planned monthly sales of 1,000 units. The monthly production plan was ramped up to 2,000 units. Orders a month after release reached 3,500 vehicles.

The manufacturer's suggested retail price (MSRP) for the Prius was set at 2.15 million yen basic, and 2.27 million yen (US$19,000–US$20,000) for a model loaded with a voice-navigation system and other extras. Other Toyota models viewed as in a comparable class at the time would have been the Carina sedan 1.5Ti, which was priced at 1.579 million yen, and the 1.6-liter Corona Premio at 1.547million yen (US$13,500–US$14,000), making the Prius conspicuously pricy for a small car, but reasonably so, considering it housed a suite of totally new components in its electric motor, generator, and large battery system. These had never before been included in any other automobile.

Prius Gets Tax Support in Japan, U.S.

The Japanese government lionized the arrival of the Prius. When a revised tax system was put in place in 1998, the government reduced taxes on new car purchases for hybrid passenger cars. The Ministry of International Trade and Industry (MITI, now the Ministry of Economy, Trade, and Industry; METI) also decided to grant consumers a subsidy for purchasing low-emission vehicles.

In the U.S., the Prius went on sale in 2000, and was astutely targeted at Hollywood celebrities who could give the car high-profile publicity. With the hope of raising the fuel-efficiency consciousness of both American consumers and automakers alike, the Internal

Revenue Service (IRS), as part of the U.S. government's 2005 energy policy, decided to issue tax credits to consumers for purchasing hybrid vehicles. The Prius received the highest credit among hybrids on the market, at US$3,150 and became the best-selling hybrid vehicle in the U.S., even after other automakers followed suit with hybrid models of their own. In 2006 alone, sales were more than double that of the next best hybrid seller from Honda.

A revision in the tax code for 2006 stipulated that the full tax credit would only be available up until the point that Toyota sold its 60,000th car. With the Prius flying off new-car lots, it didn't take long for Toyota to reach that mark.

MSRPs for 2007 Toyota- and Lexus-brand hybrids were US$22,175 for the Prius, US$25,900 for the Camry Hybrid, US$42,580 for the luxury SUV, Lexus RX 400 Hybrid, and US$54,900 for the luxury sedan, Lexus GS 450 Hybrid.

By October 2006, the tax credit for Toyota hybrid vehicles sold in the U.S. had been graduated down to half its original value at US$1,575, and was slated to disappear completely by 2008. But regardless of the existence of a tax credit, Toyota remained bullish about its sales, and didn't see as necessary a strategy to lure customers through discounts and heaps of incentives.

2007 Toyota Camry Hybrid
Photograph sourced from public domain.

The federal and state governments implemented a variety of tax benefits or special incentives to get people to switch to hybrids and other low-emission vehicles. Some states, such as California, allowed single drivers of hybrids to use the carpool lanes normally reserved for vehicles carrying two or more passengers. But even with the repeal of some of these measures, sales of Toyota hybrid vehicles have remained strong.

The New Prius

After the release of the first-generation Prius, the engineers at Toyota continued to improve it. By 2003, Toyota was ready to release an all-new, second-generation Prius—bigger and better across the board and providing significantly higher power performance. The emergence of a high-performance hybrid vehicle harbored the potential of expanding the Prius customer base from the "eco-conscious" or "first adopter" consumer to general car owners everywhere.

1997 Prius
Photograph courtesy of Toyota Motor Corp.

The decisive factor for the new Prius was a new and improved battery called the Hybrid Synergy Drive concept. The addition of a boost converter more than doubled battery voltage, increasing power to the motor without having to increase the size of the battery, or stack more batteries into the system. This allowed engineers to pursue more compact battery technology while still improving power.

To elaborate, the motor-propulsion batteries used in Toyota's hybrid cars are "modular," meaning they consist of

2004 Prius
Photograph courtesy of Toyota Motor Corp.

"modules" of six small batteries stacked together. These modules are then linked to achieve the high voltage needed to power the motor. If one hopes to get high voltage with a battery, there's a need to string together a lot of cells, adding significant weight to the vehicle.

"Making the battery lightweight and able to fit into a small space was a monumental headache," recalls Panasonic EV Energy president Yuichi Fujii.

But adding the boost converter to the new Prius let Toyota engineers reduce the battery weight while increasing power to the motor. This comes in handy on the freeway, or when one needs sudden acceleration up a hill, because the raised voltage supplies that extra muscle the motor needs to rotate the wheels.

In addition to the electric motor, improvements were made to the engine and generator to the point where the car could run on just the engine, motor, and generator even if the battery was to run out of juice.

The new Prius housed the same four-cylinder, 1.5-liter engine as its predecessor, but had been made much more powerful. Moreover, motor dimensions remained the same, but output swelled from 30 kilowatts to 50 kilowatts, leading to more than 10 percent gains in maximum output and more than 25 percent increase in torque. The catalog data for the Prius lists an achievable fuel efficiency of 35.5 kilometers per liter (83.5 miles per gallon), and the cabin was designed to seat a family comfortably.

Despite this new Prius being much easier to drive, the sticker price was frozen at first-generation levels six years prior, undoubtedly a major reason the new Prius has so far outpaced sales of the first Prius by three times. Toyota sold 125,750 units of the 2004 Prius, tripling the previous year's sales. In 2005, the figure rose further to 175,150 vehicles.

Because of refinements in performance and size, it was now possible to deploy the hybrid system to other platforms as well, such as the Estima (Previa), Lexus RX, and Kluger (Highlander). With the surging demand for hybrid vehicles, Toyota expanded its primary base of production from its world headquarters plant in Toyota city to regional factories. Production began on hybrid versions of the Lexus RX and Highlander in March 2005 at Toyota Motor Kyushu, Inc., in Fukuoka prefecture, where one of every three cars churned out on the assembly line is now a hybrid. Above the line is a gold-plated plaque emblazoned with the Lexus motto: "The Relentless Pursuit of Perfection."

Weighing in at a hefty 176 pounds, the electric motor for hybrids has to be loaded onto the production line by an automatic conveyor. A bright orange, high-tension cable attached to the battery uncoils itself in a wire harness. "We have to tread very carefully when entering the engine room so as not to step on it or get tangled up in it," says Haku Yamashita, technical chief of assembly at the Miyata Plant in Kyushu. "With a battery emitting 280 volts of DC electricity, which the inverter then modulates into 650 volts of AC electricity, we have to invent ways to protect ourselves from any chance of electrocution."

Toyota Group Decentralizes into Specialties

The Prius and other hybrid successes have increased the level of product specialization among Toyota group companies and suppliers such as Aisin Seiki Co. and Denso Corporation. Aisin AW Co. (located in Aichi prefecture), a subsidiary of Aisin Seiki, began producing key components for Lexus hybrid cars in 2006.

Because the Lexus must be able to reach speeds of 155 miles per hour, it needs to be more powerful than the Prius. But because the motor can't be increased in size, Aisin AW has designed a two-stage motor-reduction device to secure power at a relatively low cost. After its successful deployment with the Lexus GS 450h hybrid, Aisin AW was commissioned to produce hybrid system transmissions and major components for the Escape, Ford's first production hybrid, after the American automaker entered into a licensing agreement in 2004 to use technology that had been patented by Toyota.

Denso, too, saw its orders rise for inverters used in the Prius and the Lexus RX, prompting a full-scale reorganization of the company, which resulted in a new electric systems business group to handle automotive electrical products, particularly hybrid electric vehicle (HEV) components. HEV division chief Yoshihito Yamada sees a future of business expansion ahead. "We got a good jump on producing power-control units for batteries, but now I see us moving into electric motors in the near future as well."

Troubleshooting the Prius

In May 2005, a problem arose that took some of the wind out of Prius sales. Phone lines at the U.S. National Highway Traffic Safety Administration (NHTSA) were becoming clogged with callers complaining that their vehicles had stalled on the road. An investigation was launched.

The problem was pinpointed to a certain percentage of 2004 and 2005 models. The number of publicly announced cases started at 13, but swelled from there. Because none of these had resulted in injury or death, Toyota initially balked at the idea of a recall.

But not wanting to risk damaging their soaring image and public trust in the safety and reliability of their hybrid car, Toyota management sent in about 200 software technicians to cooperate with the NHTSA, and discover the source of the problem. The Prius had become key to Toyota's global growth strategy and to its new image around the world as a greener, forward-thinking company. That kind of brand capital must not be lost.

As Expected, a Software Glitch

Ultimately, by October, Toyota discovered the problems were due to, yes, a software glitch, related to control of the gasoline engine. Toyota initiated a recall to repair free of charge the firmware on some 160,000 vehicles worldwide that had been manufactured between 2004 and 2005.

"The hybrid system is all about computer controls," noted Toyota engineering advisor Hiroyuki Watanabe, who took part in the Prius' launch.

Computers are built into every pivotal bit of machinery in a hybrid car, and like the planetary gear that splits power between the gas engine and electric motor, the whole system is fused and interlocked by the system-control software. It holds the key to the car's performance reliability. "A tiny software glitch" may not seem like much, but can become the chink in the armor that compromises the safety of the entire vehicle.

The timing of the problem when it surfaced, too, was ominous. The Japanese government had just slapped an embargo on the import of American beef to Japan, citing insufficient efforts on the part of the U.S. Department of Agriculture (USDA) to ensure that beef was not tainted with BSE, or "mad cow disease." Citing the measure as an overreaction, Agriculture Secretary Mike Johanns criticized it by asking whether the U.S. would be justified in sealing its borders to all Japanese cars if just one vehicle was found to have faulty brakes.

The Prius incident—as well as the beef issue—was ultimately resolved, but public sentiment can turn on a dime, and Toyota had learned not to take anything for granted. The Prius had contributed to Toyota's growing footprint in the U.S. market, particularly in terms of image, and represented an immense threat to rival automakers. As mentioned earlier, GM has had a joint partnership with Toyota since 1984 in NUMMI, an automobile manufacturing plant in Fremont, California, where both companies share technology to produce cars. They've also collaborated on another venture in environmental tech-

2008 Prius
Photograph courtesy of Toyota Motor Corp.

nology research since 1999. But as Toyota gained strength in this area through the hybrid, it began to exclude future technology development projects, such as hybrid electric and fuel-cell vehicles from the list of joint efforts, clearly demonstrating that it needed to profit from the gains it had made in the kinds of technologies that would shape the automotive industry in the future. With a counteroffensive surely coming, Toyota knew, thanks in large part to its president, Okuda, that it must remain on the move at all times.

The Pitfalls of Rapid Expansion

The dangers of complacency were, indeed, brought home further in the summer of 2006. Toyota was hit by a storm of controversy over quality. According to a report by Japan's Ministry of Land, Infrastructure, and Transport, the number of recalls Toyota had made domestically had been rising rapidly since 2001, reaching a historic high in 2005, and affecting some 1.9 million vehicles. That was in stark contrast to major domestic rivals Nissan and Honda, which had seen their number of recalls dropping. The number of recalled vehicles in the U.S. had also swollen.

Toyota chairman Fujio Cho had sounded the alarm, having just been named chairman of the Japan Automobile Manufacturers Association (JAMA): "I think it's a case of our eyes not reaching everywhere. Rapid globalization and increased production have left us short on manpower and more reliant on procurement from outside component makers. We need to improve our field of vision to better grasp the quality control situation."

Current Toyota president Katsuaki Watanabe chimed in at the announcement of fiscal results for 2005, held in May of 2006, his head bowed at the podium in apology for the quality woes that had befallen the company. "Quality is our lifeblood. It is the president's role to solve this important question, and I will make it my number one priority in our policy for the new fiscal year." In June, Watanabe posted a second executive vice president in charge of quality assurance where previously there had been only one, as well as a senior manager.

The rapid expansion of production was certainly one of the major reasons behind the problem. Toyota was responding to rapidly increasing demand for its products in the global marketplace by expanding local production and building new business bases overseas. Toyota had seen the need to merge platforms to lower costs, and share components across platforms, and they had done so aggressively. Design, too, had gone digital to promote coordinated workflows. But that also meant that one small defect anywhere in the world could set off a chain reaction, and expand exponentially. Hybrid production also warranted special vigilance, particularly as more group subsidiaries began taking part in the production and supply chain.

"Since when did Toyota get like this? We've always been known for not making rash decisions, being very deliberate about a decision, but then executing with dispatch once made.

That's the Toyota way," said honorary chairman Shoichiro Toyoda at a board meeting to discuss his long-term strategy, Global Master Plan, in response to what he felt was a hastily executed expansion drive.

At a new year's gathering of JAMA at the start of 2007, Toyoda was heard to whisper, "What's the rush to surpass GM? If we do, we'll lose one of our biggest targets."

"Our recent models come off the line in exceptional shape. That's not the problem. And we've gotten over the hurdle of ensuring quality in auto depreciation," added executive vice president Masatami Takimoto. Right now, Toyota's impassioned effort to restore trust in its quality is beginning to produce its intended results. But as a popular saying goes in Japanese, "inattention is forbidden."

Chapter 2

Honda's Green Offensive

Fukui Gives Chase to Toyota

Honda President Takeo Fukui was visibly in high spirits, his face beaming with confidence. "Honda will take the leadership in diesel-car technology," he declared. "Our engineers may have gotten off to a late start in developing diesel technology, but they are going great guns now."

Takeo Fukui
Photograph courtesy of Honda Motor Co.

Unusually verbose, Fukui was glowing about his company's rapid progress in developing next-generation green technologies. "The principal challenge facing the auto industry in the twenty-first century is how to make cars cleaner, and that's where we'll be concentrating our technological resources. We are making great strides not only in hybrids but also in fuel-cell cars."

Fukui's exuberance fit the occasion. He was talking to a legion of auto critics and journalists at Honda Technical Reviews 2006, a big media event held on September 22, 2006, at Honda's sprawling R&D center in Haga, Tochigi prefecture.

Looking quite comfortable in his lab coat, Fukui hosted the event to show off a panoply of technologies designed to put Honda at the forefront of the ecological revolution in car manufacturing for the twenty-first century. He paraded a whole range of next-generation power-train technologies set to achieve Honda's self-imposed CO_2 reduction targets across all products and production activities around the world by the 2010 deadline.

Honda's future fleet of eco-friendly vehicles were all on proud display: a vehicle powered by a super-clean diesel engine, a next-generation fuel-cell concept (FCX), and an ethanol car. Guests were then generously invited to test drive these vehicles to their heart's content on a 4,600-yard course.

Breakthrough Emission-Control Technology

But it was the next-generation diesel engine that served as the centerpiece of the Honda tech show. The engine was billed as so clean that it would sweep away all diesel doubters, thanks to a newly developed dual-layer catalyst. The catalyst worked to sharply curtail NO_x emissions using internally produced ammonia that reduces NO_x to plain nitrogen. Honda claimed it to be first such system of its kind in the world. Indeed, the engine had satisfied U.S. emissions regulations, which required that diesel engines emit the same or lower NO_x levels as gasoline engines.

Briefly, the NO_x catalyst absorbs NO_x from the exhaust stream, and produces ammonia by allowing hydrogen obtained from the exhaust stream to react with the absorbed NO_x. Then the catalyst temporarily absorbs the ammonia, and uses it to reduce NO_x to nitrogen. This innovation led to the development of a compact and light exhaust-purification system for diesel engines. The new system showed improved purification performance at temperatures between 200°C and 300°C: the main temperature range for diesel engines.

Honda plans to make further improvements on this technology to develop a diesel engine that can fulfill the Tier 2 Bin 1 regulations, due to be introduced in the U.S. in 2009. The new regulations demand near-zero emissions. The hope is to launch passenger vehicles powered by the new super-clean diesel engine in the U.S. within three years, as the first step in a global diesel offensive.

"If we can meet the world's most stringent diesel exhaust standards adopted by the U.S., we can sell our diesel vehicles anywhere in the world," Fukui said, sounding a lot like Daimler's Dieter Zetsche.

In 2003, Honda started full-scale production of the diesel-powered Accord in its plant in the U.K. The car's combustion controls were improved by optimizing the combustion chamber configuration and shortening the injection time by way of a "common-rail" system that generates injection pressures of up to 2,000 bar. The diesel engine offers higher horsepower while emitting less NO_x and soot. The engine clears tough Euro 4 emissions standards, and has been mounted in both the Civic and CR-V models as well.

In 2005, diesel vehicles accounted for about 30 percent of Honda's annual sales of 250,000 units in Europe. But the company has kept working to develop even cleaner diesel engines for the markets in the U.S. and Japan, where diesel exhaust regulations are much tighter.

"Honda will continue pursuing hybrid technology, but this new diesel engine will be spearheading our clean-car line," noted Fukui.

Next-Generation Fuel-Cell Concept

Honda's next-generation fuel-cell vehicle, the "FCX Concept," drew plenty of interest at the technical review, particularly since it was shown running. A newly developed fuel-cell stack, smaller and more efficient than any in the past, boasted dramatic environmental and driving performance. With its spacious interior and capsule-like aerodynamic design, the concept truly embodies Honda's vision of the future for clean-running passenger cars. Also on display was an older version of the FCX, which in 2002 was test-driven by then Prime Minister Junichiro Koizumi, and delivered to the prime minister's office. But it had been a boxy minivan, and it was clear that Honda had made great progress in downsizing the fuel-cell power train.

In the traditional fuel-cell stack, water formed during electricity generation flows through the system horizontally. But in the new Honda fuel-cell platform, water flows vertically. This has led to a 20 percent reduction in volume and a 30 percent reduction in weight. With maximum power output increased by 14 kilowatts, the fuel-cell system is both powerful and compact.

The power output of the drive motor has also increased by 15 kilowatts. The front end of the vehicle has been shortened by aligning the motor with the gearbox. The onboard power plant is 180 kilograms lighter and 40 percent smaller than that of the current FCX, freeing up significant room for the cabin.

Honda displayed the FCX Concept at the 2007 Detroit Auto Show, and plans to start leasing the vehicle in Japan and the U.S. in 2008.

In May 2007, Honda announced bold CO_2 reduction targets for all its products and production activities around the world. According to Fukui, the initiative is driven by a strong conviction that as a "facilitator of mobility," selling products to more than 21 million customers each year, Honda has an obligation to minimize the impact of its operations on the environment.

"Just as we once pioneered clean gasoline-engine technology by developing the CVCC, we are determined to demonstrate our leadership again with the evolution of diesel-engine technology," Fukui proclaimed.

"Honda has always emphasized originality and high aims. As environmental issues assume greater importance in the coming years, we will do more than pursue cleaner technologies. We will create world-beating technologies that are built into a superlative ride, and provide the greatest driving pleasure without ever compromising on environmental performance."

Honda's Green Legacy

Until Toyota launched the Prius in 1997, Honda had become widely viewed as the industry's leader in environmental technology. In 1971, when founder Soichiro Honda was president, Honda catapulted itself to world dominance in low-emission engines by announcing the development of its groundbreaking CVCC technology. After its commercialization, Honda turned around, and made this innovative emission-control technology widely available

First generation Honda Civic
Photograph courtesy of Honda Motor Co.

to automakers around the world, so that it would gain international recognition. The new CVCC engine powered a spunky new passenger compact called the Honda Civic, and became an instant hit because of its low emissions and high mileage. CVCC was the innovation that placed Honda squarely alongside its Japanese rivals, Toyota and Nissan, in the U.S. auto market.

Emissions Standards in the U.S.

As with Toyota, Honda's CVCC project was prompted by U.S. legislation. The *Clean Air Act 1970*, which revised the existing *Clean Air Act 1963* to introduce far more stringent emissions standards, required lowering automobile emissions of CO, HC, and NO_x to one-tenth of current levels, starting with models made in 1975 (CO, HC) and 1976 (NO_x). Japanese automakers scrambled to develop vehicles that could meet the new standards, but it was widely believed that the emissions targets were unachievable. Honda, ironically the last Japanese company to enter the auto business, pulled off a major coup with a technological miracle ahead of its rivals.

It was a feat a long time in the making for then Honda president Soichiro Honda. Back in the early 1960s, he had fulminated against MITI's initiative to promote consolidation among uncompetitive Japanese automakers, and restrict new entries into the industry. The ministry was hoping to protect the domestic auto industry from the expected onslaught of competition from powerful foreign rivals once market liberaliza-

Honda N360
Photograph courtesy of Honda Motor Co.

tions took hold. The charismatic Honda founder ordered the company's R&D section to quickly develop four-wheeled vehicles. And Honda launched its first vehicles in 1963, the T360, a light truck, and the S500, a sports car. Honda was also pressing the R&D team to develop its first small passenger car, the N360, which was rolled out in 1966. And as part of his expansion drive, Honda announced the company's entry into Formula 1 racing in 1964.

By the early 1970s, the fledgling auto company could ill afford to devote many engineers to air-pollution research, which could take many years before producing tangible results. But morale among Honda's engineers was high due to the company's expansion into the automobile market and Formula 1 racing. They were eager to take on environmental issues as well, be it in the U.S., Europe, or Japan.

Under these circumstances, in 1966, JAMA sent a fact-finding mission to the U.S. to study the kinds of pollution that automobiles were causing. The mission visited the big three automakers—GM, Ford, and Chrysler—and affiliated labs to observe what kind of research was being conducted to clean up tailpipe emissions. The answers were varied. Major U.S. automakers were developing exhaust-control technologies, such as catalytic mufflers, exhaust-gas recirculation (EGR) systems, and lean-burn systems. But just as with the 80 or so hybrid choices Toyota designers had considered with the Prius, nobody was sure which of these technologies should be adopted. The U.S. Motor Vehicle Manufacturers Association (MVMA) proposed joint research among U.S., Japanese, and European manufacturers. But the idea failed to materialize because of concerns about possible antitrust violations.

Soichiro Honda Grows Wildly Optimistic

After receiving a report on the mission's findings, Hideo Sugiura, the chief of Honda's R&D center, decided that the company would do best to develop its own proprietary tailpipe solutions. So Sugiura set up the Air Pollution Control Research Lab, or AP Lab, specifically for that task. The engineers assigned to the new team had previously spent all their time studying ways to make engines more powerful, and had no experience with emissions control. They had to start with the basics. Practically the only machine available to them at the time was an instrument to measure CO. They had no idea what NO_x or HC even meant, much less the equipment to measure these gases. Initially, they used a device called a gas chromatograph to measure the components of exhaust gas by observing color reactions to chemical reagent. But this method caused the engine condition to change during measurements, making it impossible for researchers to apply their findings.

Yet Soichiro Honda grew wildly optimistic about the work at the AP Lab. "For Honda, the last to enter the market for four-wheel vehicles, this is a great opportunity to be on the leading edge with other companies," he said, in a pep talk to engineers. The Honda founder, a savvy mechanical engineer himself, offered various suggestions for the lab, including the promotion of fuel vaporization during intake using a new mechanism, and the maintenance of proper intake through a fuel-injection system.

"Mr. Honda came to the lab every morning to check on progress, and offer ideas," recalled Fukui, who at the time was one of the youngest engineers in the lab. "He once told me to study whether a torch engine could be used to remove NO_x. I worked all night to design such an engine, but it was too big to be mounted in a car. The next day, I sheepishly told him the results. Realizing I'd been up all night grappling with it, he merely nodded, said 'No problem,' and walked away." The effort had been noted.

The AP Lab began with Honda researchers experimenting with various measures for emission controls that their rivals were testing, as well as conducting their own surveys and research. The lab also looked into the causes of photochemical smog in the U.S., and examined efforts and initiatives to curb vehicle-caused pollution there. Studies were conducted on a broad array of possible emissions-control technologies: improvements in gasoline- and diesel-engine technologies, alternatives such as gas turbines and rotary engines, post-processing devices such as oxidation catalysts and thermal reactors, and alternative fuels such as alcohol and hydrogen.

After extensive research on potential candidates, the Honda development team decided to focus on developing a lean-burning engine. Although use of post-processing devices seemed at first the easiest way, the engineers ultimately concluded that a better approach was to try improving the combustion engine to make exhausts cleaner.

This was the idea that emerged from discussions between Honda researchers and Tsuyoshi Asanuma, then a University of Tokyo professor who was acting as an adviser for the lab. They became convinced that the only realistic way to reduce CO, HC, and NO_x emissions at the same time was the adoption of a lean-combustion method to burn the fuel more completely. But this presented a challenge that was beyond the technological standards of the time. Again, Soichiro Honda arrived on the scene to put things in simple perspective. "You'll never know unless you try, right?"

They conducted tests on every conceivable idea: heating the air-fuel mixture, reinforcing the gas movement in the cylinder, increasing the ignition energy, multiple ignitions with several spark plugs, and so forth. But none of the tests produced promising results.

After a while, the researchers came to realize that they were unlikely to achieve a breakthrough by simply trying the same ideas that had been studied by other automakers. Once they began trying to think outside the box, somebody came up with the idea to build a special "pre-chamber" off the main combustion chamber—an approach no other company seemed to have pursued, but just might work.

An air-fuel mixture that was low in fuel could not be ignited by a spark plug. So Honda found a two-pronged process. First, a rich mixture was ignited in a pre-chamber, and then the flame generated was used to ignite a lean mixture in the main combustion chamber.

Some diesel units at that time were equipped with pre-chambers, and research was under way in the Soviet Union to achieve a similar process using a gasoline engine to capitalize on low-grade fuel, or improve fuel economy. But the Honda engineers thought it might be possible to use this method to control air pollution as well, and started research on use of this pre-chamber to develop a cleaner-burning gasoline engine.

They quickly found to their dismay, however, that there were a host of technological hurdles to overcome to ensure that a lean-burn engine with a pre-chamber could work in a stable and reliable manner.

Having no patience to wait for a prototype engine to be manufactured, Soichiro Honda suggested that the company's general-purpose engines that already had pre-chambers in them be used for the research. A series of tests were carried out on the GD90 general-purpose diesel engine, which was a two-cylinder, V-type 479-cc diesel unit with a pre-chamber.

First, the researchers installed a spark plug and a gasoline-injection nozzle into the pre-chamber, remodeling the engine to allow the adjustment of pressure ratios. The results of tests using the remodeled engine proved promising. In the meantime, a trial-manufactured version of the single-cylinder, 30cc N600 engine was completed, and the team immediately began trying to determine the optimal pre-chamber conditions for it.

It was then that Soichiro chimed in again with another suggestion. "Why not use the mechanical fuel-injection system we developed recently?" This led to the decision to study two fuel-supply methods: fuel injection and carburetion.

Next, the team had to embark on research on water-cooled engines, which were essential for efficient exhaust control. But Honda didn't have a water-cooled automotive engine that could be used for testing. So it decided to conduct tests using 1.6-liter engines built by Nissan, and units of other competitors.

"Leaving People Upstairs and Taking Down the Ladder"

Subsequent research using the N600 engine resulted in a palpable reduction of toxic substances. Upon hearing the news, Soichiro Honda jumped to his feet and declared he would make a public announcement about their low-emission engine. Just as Uchiyamada's team reacted to management's hurried approach for the Prius, the Honda researchers, who were still processing their patent applications, were taken aback by the president's declaration, but had to accept the decision by their revered founder. The engineers decided to create an abstruse name for the new engine that didn't give any hint about its structure.

Honda's new low-emission engine technology was dubbed CVCC, or Compound Vortex Controlled Combustion. "Compound" represented the engine mechanism, with two combustion chambers: main and auxiliary, while "vortex" referred to the swirl generated in the main chamber. Created by a jet of flame from the pre-chamber injected via a nozzle, the vortex boosted the speed of engine combustion. "Controlled Combustion" described the engine's ability to control the speed or rate of combustion properly.

In justifying his reason for announcing the engine before its completion, Honda told his engineers, "If I asked you guys when it would be completed, you would most likely always say, 'not quite yet.' The company would go bankrupt before that."

This was vintage Soichiro Honda, a man who was often said to employ a tactic of "leaving people upstairs and then taking down the ladder." His decision to announce the engine fit that description. It was designed to stimulate progress in the research and, hopefully, boost morale by providing a common goal toward which to work.

At a press conference held on February 12, 1971, at the Federation of Economic Organizations Hall in Tokyo's business district of Otemachi, the hard-driving Honda president said, "We are developing a reciprocating engine that meets [U.S.] emissions standards for 1975. And we will commence production of it in 1973."

Still, there were many technological challenges that had to be sorted out. First of all, Honda researchers had to prove that the technical concept of an engine with a pre-chamber would work in an actual automobile. The new engine was to be installed in the Civic, a small passenger car then under development. Although the engine displacement had been determined with that vehicle in mind, it became clear from available data and simulations that a two-liter CVCC engine would be needed to meet tough U.S. emissions standards.

The first prototype engine was produced in great haste. After bench tests to check basic performance, the prototype units were installed in Nissan Sunny bodies for field tests.

Pre-chamber-based lean combustion did reduce CO, NO_x, and HC, but the HC reduction performance didn't measure up to the 1975 standards of the *Clean Air Act 1970*. Subsequent research on the manifold emissions system, however, combined with the right combination of a main chamber, a pre-chamber, and a fuel-supply method led to the desired oxidation reaction in the exhaust pipe through heat present in the exhaust gas. This improved HC reduction performance, paving the way for Honda's groundbreaking engine to satisfy U.S. standards without the need for a catalytic converter.

CVCC Establishes Honda as Green

On October 11, 1972, Honda presented all its hitherto "veiled" details about the CVCC to a huge crowd of journalists from all over the world, who packed a hall at Tokyo's Akasaka Prince Hotel. The entire Honda management team was present, including president Soichiro Honda, along with the other directors and engineers involved in the project. They introduced the engine, ran everybody through a brief history of its evolution, and described its features and combustion principles.

Honda executives explained why the CVCC engine was such a great achievement. The new system could be made using existing reciprocating engine technology, which meant that current production facilities could be used. Since the only major change required was the replacement of a portion of the cylinder head, the system could be easily applied elsewhere. And because it ensured clean, complete combustion internally, additional devices such as catalytic converters were rendered unnecessary. The message was clear: Honda's new low-emission engine was a marvelous wonder of innovation that would certainly revolutionize automotive engines.

It was feted as a landmark day in the history of the latecomer Japanese auto manufacturer. The hall was even decked out in blue panels to represent a clear blue sky. With this engine, Honda could claim world leadership in environmental technology.

As expected, the announcement did cause a worldwide stir. The EPA asked Honda to submit a sampling of cars equipped with the CVCC engine for testing. Honda sent three CVCC-powered vehicles to the EPA's laboratory in Ann Arbor, Michigan. Durability testing on these units was conducted in the presence of Honda executives in December 1972. The vehicles passed, becoming the first to meet the stringent 1975 emissions requirements of the *Clean Air Act 1970*.

As Honda offered the technology for use by other automakers, Toyota responded quickly and signed a licensing agreement with Honda by the end of the year. Soon, Honda's R&D center started receiving visitors from major automakers around the world. Licensing agreements were eventually signed with Ford, Chrysler, and Isuzu.

On March 19, 1973, the EPA held a public hearing in Washington, D.C., to hear the testimony of automakers to decide whether the *Clean Air Act 1970* should be put into effect as scheduled. At the hearing, only two automakers said they could meet the regulations: Honda and Toyo Industries (now Mazda). After the hearing, the EPA decided to postpone the implementation of the *Clean Air Act*.

But the CVCC technology provided a huge thrust for Honda and its Civic car. In December 1973, the first four-door Civic CVCC went on sale in Japan. In the U.S., the EPA certified the 1975 Civic CVCC as satisfying its emissions requirements. The product not only won EPA certification, but also earned the top rating for fuel economy.

Meanwhile, Toyota was working hard to develop an exhaust-control system using a catalyst. The idea was to minimize changes to existing engine technology to maintain performance, while using a catalyst to reduce toxic emissions. Toyota was also studying ways to improve engines' environmental performance through combustion control. Lean-burn technology was developed to burn air-fuel mixtures that reduced CO, HC, and NO_x emissions. But the leanness of the gas tended to cause problems, such as failure to ignite properly and unstable burning, and posed huge hurdles to near-term commercialization.

At the end of 1973, Toyota had decided to adopt Honda's CVCC technology. But after further research and improvements were made, Toyota then opted to develop a catalyst-based system through a decision based on evaluations of all key factors, including fuel efficiency, driving performance, serviceability and costs.

Catalysts are very sensitive materials, and their use in automobiles under varying conditions can prove extremely difficult. Even specialized makers of catalysts could not keep up with Toyota's demands and pace of development. So Toyota began building them itself.

Amid the challenge of securing sufficient reliability, Toyota was pressed to come up with emission-control systems for all its models within a very short time. To complicate matters further, Toyota engineers had to keep tabs on how various problems and variations in individual parts would affect the reliability of the entire emission-control system.

Ultimately, Toyota adopted both the compound vortex and catalyst-based systems to enable its products to meet the 1975 emissions standards. In 1976, Toyota launched its first two standards-compliant models: the two-liter Corona and two-liter Carina.

Toyota Plays Catch-up

When the even more stringent 1976 emissions standards were announced, then Toyota president Eiji Toyoda, who headed JAMA, declared them unachievable with the technologies available. His remarks left the impression that Toyota was not very supportive of emission controls. With Honda's CVCC already established as an effective exhaust-control technology, the surging Toyota rival was solidifying its status as a new-age leader in automotive technology.

Toyota's engineers, however, continued their efforts to develop an original lean-burn system. They used electronic system analyses extensively in hopes of hitting upon the optimal package. Eventually, and much to their credit, they did succeed in developing a system that met 1976 emission standards through tenacious efforts to deal with technological problems one at a time. By installing a pre-chamber within—not outside—the main chamber, Toyota solved the two major drawbacks of a lean-burn system: poor ignition performance and unstable combustion. In another example of a small but important improvement, it changed spark-plug positioning to prevent excessive exposure to heat.

But the key innovation was the development of an O_2 sensor to measure the concentration of oxygen in exhaust gas. This made it possible to keep the fuel-air ratio stabilized at a fixed level. The breakthrough cleared the way for practical use of a three-way catalytic device that reduced CO, HC, and NO_x emissions at the same time.

Since the electrodes of sensors were exposed to high-temperature exhaust gas, it was difficult to give them the durability they needed. Constant exposure to high temperatures tended to cause the electrodes to fall off and break sensory elements. Toyota worked with a parts supplier, Denso Corporation, to design and develop a structure that would make sensors heat-resistant. Close cooperation between development and production engineers resulted in the achievement of high-performance, highly durable O_2 sensors.

Toyota's all-out effort to clean up tailpipe emissions bore fruit in the forms of the Crown 2000 and Mark II 2000, which were launched in June 1977. Equipped with a three-way catalytic converter, these models met 1978 emission standards. Toyota also developed its turbulence generating pot (TGP) combustion system and an oxidation catalytic converter as a lean-burn technology. These innovations led to more models that met the 1978 emissions standards, including the flagship model, the Corolla. At last, Toyota had caught up with Honda in green technology.

But Honda again raced ahead, improving the gas mileage of its Civic CVCC year after year. For four straight years until its 1978 model, Civic maintained the title of the most fuel-efficient vehicle in the U.S. And the Civic earned widespread recognition among American consumers as the paragon of a low-emissions, fuel-efficient car.

When the *Clean Air Act 1970* went into force in 1975, Toyota and other automakers responded with such measures as equipping their cars with oxidation catalytic devices. But oxidation catalysts were costly because they required a large amount of expensive platinum. Pre-chamber based systems still retained many advantages over oxidation catalytic devices.

Eventually, the CVCC system was superseded by new innovations like the three-way catalytic system or electronic fuel injection. But this technology powered Honda's advance into the front ranks of green-car manufacturing. By tackling a technological challenge that was seen by most automakers as impossible to overcome, and succeeding in developing technology that radically raised the efficiency of automotive engines, Honda earned a great social reputation as an eco-conscious automaker. In the U.S., in particular, Honda's stature as a viable four-wheel-car manufacturer rose sharply, triggering the company's drive to establish a powerful network of dealerships in the world's largest car market.

One notable factor behind the Honda CVCC story is found in a practice called *waigaya*, a term created from two Japanese words used to describe a noisy crowd. "We at Honda often use the word to describe the atmosphere at the lab," recalls Sugiura, who headed the research center. "Three or four people would often gather in a small room, drink coffee, and chat noisily about the future and their ambitions. Through such informal rap sessions, problems and issues would surface, and often a consensus emerged that something should be done to address them." Sugiura maintains that quick responses to social trends are crucial for long-term success, if not for short-term profits. "This is an important factor for a company's long-term viability and growth."

Beaten to the Punch

Boosted by its success with the Civic, Honda made its next big drive to create a zero-emissions vehicle from the late 1980s to early 1990s, when calls for tighter emission controls resurfaced amid concerns about global warming.

Honda's response was to first embark on the development of a practical EV. At a meeting held at their headquarters, management discussed how the company should respond to such key environmental challenges as the development of "clean energy" technologies and preparation for eventual depletion or phasing out of fossil fuels. They realized that EVs had fewer parts than conventional automobiles, which meant they could be manufactured more easily anywhere in the world. They also reconfirmed the need to advance the internal combustion engine further for better gas mileage and lower emissions. Honda's research managers agreed in the end that the EV held the most promise of all alternative-fuel vehicles under consideration.

But once again, Honda had no previous experience in developing electric power drives. There was no palpable research into alternative-fuel vehicles under way at Honda at that time. In April 1988, a small team of just four people was formed to conduct basic research on EVs. It was by no means early on this initiative, because many auto manufacturers both at home and abroad were already developing their own EVs.

One major and inherent technological challenge lay in the power output of a battery being far smaller than the amount of energy displaced by gasoline combustion. And it simply takes too many hours to recharge a battery. So using a battery to power a vehicle would have to mean enormous compromises on performance and convenience. Golf carts and amusement-park rides were almost the only EVs in use at the time.

What sets an electric car apart from a conventional gasoline-powered one is the motor and battery system. The only type of battery available for use that could conceivably power an automobile at the time was a lead-acid unit. The development of a better battery for use in vehicles would require several years.

Despite all these problems, however, Honda researchers started producing an EV prototype using the Civic CR-X as the base. In 1991, the first prototype was completed. Both the motor and the battery were products available on the market because there was not enough time to develop them from scratch. Aluminum was used for the body and acrylic for glass to make the vehicle as light as possible. Honda's first EV proved a product of painful labor. Because of many technological shortcomings, it was not something proud Honda engineers were ready to badge a fully fledged Honda automobile, and the vehicle was roundly criticized.

EV Development Project with Two Objectives in Focus

Learning some lessons from that shaky start, Honda researchers made a renewed commitment to developing a really strong EV without succumbing to compromise. Honda decided to open the throttle in creating a commercially viable EV. One of the first tasks engineers tackled was changing the battery specifications to better meet the needs of an EV. They studied the issue meticulously, and proposed to battery makers a format and size they thought suitable for use in an EV. Next they decided to pursue in-house manufacturing of the motor and control devices, which were the equivalent of an engine in a gasoline-powered vehicle. After considering all the relevant factors, Honda's project team chose a DC brushless motor for their EV, although it was at the time an unusual choice for a large motor. Still, test simulations had shown this type of motor to be the most efficient.

Through a process of trial and error, Honda engineers managed to develop most of the core technologies they needed for their EV. So management upgraded the project to the D stage, or production-oriented status, in June 1992. There were two conceptual goals for the project if it was to result in the best EV in the world. The vehicle should "express a clean, quiet and smooth ride that is of another dimension," and be "singularly advanced." Even at this stage, however, the prototype had a driving range of merely 25–31 miles, and there was no solution in sight to the question of how to secure sufficient impact protection for the heavy battery. In short, the prototype was far from a real-world release.

Honda EV Plus
*Photograph courtesy of
Honda Motor Co.*

Despite having to grapple with various technological problems, Honda began preparations for test driving the EV to gather actual market data in the U.S. In 1994, after signing a contract with a Californian power company, Honda began two-year test-drive programs. Before these vehicles actually hit the roads, however, it had to conduct various safety tests. One test involved applying a load of force several dozen times greater than the highest possible level that could be generated in nature to the battery and other parts. A huge amount of hydrogen gas was exploded to see whether sufficient safety could be secured both inside and outside the vehicle.

In the U.S., EV prototypes based on the Civic were used in test drives that covered a total of 80,000 miles. The tests found that the lead-acid batteries used in these cars could deteriorate very quickly when left in the summer heat for a week or two. This made it clear that the battery had to be switched to a stress-resistant NiMH type. So Honda got busy with joint development of this relatively new battery technology.

In January 1996, after test-driving a newly minted Honda EV, then president Nobuhiko Kawamoto held up his thumb and uttered, "It's a go." In April that year, Honda announced the development of its first EV in both Japan and the U.S. Almost exactly a year later, in April 1997, the Honda EV Plus rolled off the production line at the company's Takanezawa Plant in Tochigi prefecture, marking the start of commercial production for the vehicle.

Even as it rolled off the line, there remained many problems to be solved. The vehicle was heavy and expensive because of the 1,100-pound battery, which could power the car for only a short distance per charge. Its practical utility was poor, and low prices at the pump weren't helping to raise the profile of EVs, either.

Against this backdrop, Honda started seriously considering the idea of developing a hybrid car, using an electric motor that could help a car wring more miles out of a tank of gas. Honda had long been exploring hybrid technology as a means to boost fuel efficiency while developing EV technology, and the company's quest for fuel economy had already produced some notable achievements, such as the VTEC engine.

A Two-Seater Hybrid Project

In the late 1980s, Honda was working on what it dubbed a "next-generation engine." The effort led to the completion in 1989 of the Variable Valve Timing and Lift Electronic Control (VTEC) engine, which generated far greater horsepower per gallon than previous engines for a remarkable improvement in gas mileage.

Next, Honda launched a new project codenamed CR-X to develop a two-seater sports car with a light, aluminum-based body that could run 50 miles on a gallon of gasoline.

But hybrid technology drew the interest of the company's Formula 1 development team, which was pursuing a new approach to higher fuel economy. Unlike Toyota, Honda focused on a two-seater sports car in its hybrid project, instead of a family car that could carry four or five people. Former Honda president Kawamoto, who was involved in the project, explained that: "When we looked into the U.S. market, we found that many of the passenger cars running on highways were carrying only one or two people. So we decided to develop a two-seater car that gets great gas mileage."

Some European automakers had studied hybrid technology mainly as a means to increase the range per charge of an EV. And at the end of the 1970s, a couple of hybrid models had been announced in different parts of the globe, including VW's parallel hybrid taxi in Germany and Daihatsu's parallel hybrid truck in Japan. But enthusiasm about hybrid technology fizzled out quickly once the oil crisis was over.

When hybrid technology began attracting attention again in the 1990s, it was regarded as a technology to tackle the drawbacks of EVs. Peugeot produced its own hybrid series based on front-engine, front-wheel-drive vehicles. Volvo developed gas-turbine hybrids.

In 1993, in response to President Clinton's PNGV challenge, GM, Ford, and Chrysler chose for the program the diesel-electric parallel hybrid formula, which uses a combination of a diesel engine and an electric motor. The goal was an extremely fuel-efficient vehicle, which could get 34 kilometers per liter (80 miles per gallon), three times more fuel efficient on average than vehicles that were put on the market in 1994.

The program was terminated, though, without achieving its target for two reasons—dismal short-term prospects of developing clean diesel engines and low gas prices that were expected to keep demand for hybrid cars low. But a report on the program did point to the high potential of hybrid technology.

A hybrid car using two power sources—an internal combustion engine and an electric motor—could achieve high fuel economy because it is designed to allow the engine to stay in its most efficient load and speed range most of the time. As mentioned, to squeeze more miles out of a gallon of gasoline, a hybrid car captures some of the energy removed when the brake is applied, and stores it in the battery for later use (regenerative braking). As Toyota found out, a series of experiments had shown that hybrid technology could double a gasoline car's fuel economy without changing the fuel supply infrastructure. If nothing else, the hybrid system was recognized as a promising approach to radically improving automobile fuel economy.

It bears repeating that when the Toyota Prius is running at low speeds, the generator provides all the power needed to accelerate the car. So the vehicle needs a large and powerful generator and motor. In contrast, Honda's hybrid has an electric motor sandwiched between the engine and the transmission, and its rotor is directly linked to the engine's crankshaft. The engine and the motor form an integrated system. Since the engine is used only to provide extra power while the car is accelerating, it can be compact and simple in structure. Honda's system is sometimes called a "mild hybrid." Honda chose this system to minimize the burden of weight the motor would have on the vehicle.

Honda's Hybrid Vehicle

Honda started mass production of its first hybrid car, the Insight, in November 1999. It was a two-seater equipped with a compact 1.0-liter, three-cylinder engine. The electric motor was designed to assist the gasoline engine. The engine powered the vehicle when it ran fast, and the motor powered the car at low speeds. Electric power generated by the

Honda Insight
Photograph courtesy of Honda Motor Co.

NiMH battery assisted the gasoline engine and provided some regenerative braking to capture energy while the car was being slowed down. Honda employed its VTEC system, which reduced the engine's friction loss (engine braking power) in half, for the higher efficiency. This system was also used for the Civic Hybrid, which would replace the Insight as Honda's mainstay hybrid vehicle. The weight of the vehicle was reduced for high fuel economy through a liberal use of aluminum.

The Insight got 35 kilometers per liter (99.5 miles per gallon), the highest rating among all the mass-produced gasoline vehicles at that time. Since the gas mileage translated into 100 kilometers per three liters, Insight was promoted as a "three-liter car." It was priced at 2.1 million yen, close to the price tag of the Prius. By launching Insight in the U.S. and European markets at the same time, Honda preempted Toyota in the hybrid race overseas. Toyota had yet to launch the Prius in markets abroad.

"There were many things about our first hybrid that we didn't know for sure," recalls Akira Fujimura, a senior engineer at Honda R&D who worked on the Insight. "The battery discharged naturally, and deteriorated quickly unless recharged frequently. We also had to figure out how to prevent electrocution. And we had to carry out crash tests very meticulously."

One could say that the 1997 Kyoto Protocol to curb greenhouse gases marked the opening of a new chapter in the history of global competition among automakers to develop cleaner-running cars, particularly since the Prius debuted around the same time. The domestic launch of the Prius enabled Toyota to notch up its first victory over Honda and other rivals in the hybrid battlefront. Honda had developed hybrid technology as early as Toyota, but found itself upstaged by its big Japanese rival.

The Insight, which was slightly smaller than the 1.5-liter Prius, didn't have enough punch as a major automotive innovation. Honda's misguided marketing strategy also worked against the Insight. Toyota timed the launch of the Prius to coincide with the announcement of the Kyoto Protocol, and promoted it as a clean car. Honda, in contrast, focused on marketing its Insight as a high-mileage car. As a result, Honda allowed Toyota to steal its environmental crown. Toyota announced its five-passenger Prius before Honda did its Insight, selling it as a groundbreaking car for the next century. The level of vexation felt by Honda engineers must have been high.

Motor Fan magazine published an extra issue on November 26, 1999, featuring the Honda Insight, and announcing it as Honda's first hybrid model for the U.S. market. Its headline read that the car was surprisingly agile, and boasted a marvelous fuel economy of 35 kilometers per liter (99 miles per gallon). The article included a test-drive report and a gas-mileage test.

Indeed, the Insight was promoted as the most fuel-efficient vehicle on the market, with outstanding environmental performance, designed to offer great driving pleasure as well. But the main target was its fuel efficiency.

Honda's hybrid-development team at the firm's automobile R&D center, led by Kazuhiro Ichinose, placed as much importance on performance on the highway as that in the city. So when it was decided that the hybrid car be developed as a sports-type, front-wheel-drive, two-seater coupe, this was because this configuration offered the most lightweight and compact packaging. It sought to make the vehicle light and aerodynamically efficient, not only for higher fuel efficiency, but to achieve a styling that would evoke, as the team called it, a "refreshing cleanliness."

Kawamoto Focuses on Staying Power

If Honda's research on hybrid technology was as advanced as Toyota's, why didn't Honda try to emphasize the green and clean aspects of its hybrid car?

"We were not quite focused on promoting our image as an eco-conscious company at the time," says then president Nobuhiko Kawamoto. "Back then, we were preoccupied with restructuring our operations after the collapse of the bubble economy, efforts that made it possible for Honda to survive as a competitive company."

In 1990, as the bubble economy in Japan was bursting, and the Gulf War was depressing auto sales in the U.S., Honda changed leadership. After steering the company for seven years, Tadashi Kume resigned his post in the middle of his term, giving way to 54-year-old Kawamoto.

Born in March 1936, Kawamoto graduated from Tohoku University's Graduate School of Engineering. He joined Honda in the same year as Shoichiro Irimajiri, future vice president, and Yoshihide Munekuni, future chairman. A specialist of engine design, Kawamoto spent most of his life at Honda on R&D. He was among the engineers who learned about car manufacturing under the tutelage of founder Soichiro Honda. But Kawamoto drafted a new management credo to replace Soichiro's words, and named it the "Honda Philosophy." This was the first step in reforming the employee mindset to meet modern realities better.

"Honda of today is ill," Kawamoto declared at that time. "The way of doing business in an era when growth was the sole purpose must be replaced. My biggest role is to do away with that old convention," he said. "For Honda to become a really global company, it must not have any preset taboos. What we think is right must be expressed in clear words, and carried out without fail."

While shaking up employee thinking, Kawamoto also took steps to cut costs. He reduced the material budget, and promoted the sharing of parts among models. He also launched projects to develop such new vehicles as the Stepwagon and CR-V. These efforts paid off in the year ending March 1995, when the company reported its first growth in profits in five years. Honda's newly developed recreational vehicle (RV), the Odyssey, launched in 1995, proved a stellar hit and sparked a huge RV boom in Japan. But although Honda was capable of producing some smash hits in response to market trends, it let itself lose ground against rivals in the formation of an effective strategy to deal with a heightening environmental consciousness by consumers.

In 1998, Kawamoto was replaced by the 58-year-old Hiroyuki Yoshino, a graduate of the University of Tokyo's aeronautic engineering department. Yoshino had joined Honda because he wanted to do engine-related work. Under Yoshino, Honda increased its global sales sharply thanks to the popularity of new products like the Honda Fit subcompact. But the sales of the Insight, which hit the market after Toyota's Prius, remained sluggish, allowing Toyota to remain ahead on the environmental technology front. After five years of serving as president, Yoshino was succeeded in June 2003 by Takeo Fukui, a 58-year-old executive who had headed up Honda's R&D company.

Restoring Honda's Cachet

When he was named new acting Honda president in 2003, Fukui pledged to revive the spiritual legacy of the company's foundation. "I will pursue a vision to enhance the brand in a way consistent with Honda's corporate culture," Fukui proclaimed at a press conference.

Fukui was born in Kure, Hiroshima prefecture, on November 28, 1944. He was the youngest of the three sons born to his father, Shizuo, and mother, Momoko. A military technical officer specializing in shipbuilding, his father was building military vessels at the naval shipyard in Kure. He was involved in the construction of the *Yamato*, the legendary World War II battleship. After the end of the war, his family moved to Tokyo, where he finished his primary and secondary education.

Takeo Fukui was an avid car buff even as a child. He still remembers being thrilled at riding a scooter in an amusement park as a grade-school student. After entering junior high, his eldest brother, four years older, bequeathed to him a motor-assisted bicycle. During his high-school years, Fukui could be seen puttering about everywhere in a 50cc motorbike and then a mini-vehicle.

In 1964, Fukui entered the applied chemistry department of Waseda University's school of science and engineering. He revered Madame Curie, and his grand ambition was to win a Nobel Prize in chemistry. But Fukui's university life was spent mostly as a devoted member of the automobile club. He was confident that he was a better driver than his senior students, but as a freshman, he was given little opportunity to prove it. Instead, as did every other freshman, he had to do all the menial work, such as washing, scrubbing, and servicing cars. In summer training camps in Karuizawa, a wooded resort in Nagano prefecture, the new club members were put through rigorous physical workouts of long-distance running, pushups, sit-ups, and squat-hopping. Unable to endure the harsh training, some freshmen escaped from the camp under cover of night. But Fukui, who hated to admit defeat, stayed until the end. When he was entrusted with the management of the club in his junior year, Fukui abolished the elements of the camp that he regarded as meaningless "hazing" such as kneeling in the formal *seiza* (sitting on one's knees) position on gravel. Fukui reformed the club's "fraternity rat" culture to refocus its activity on improving members' driving skills.

In his senior year, Fukui grew so preoccupied with club activity that he found little time to attend classes for his graduation thesis. Since skipping a thesis class was strictly banned, Fukui decided to repeat the year. But his true aim may have been to win the triple crown at a driving contest among universities in the Kanto region, namely, victories in all three events of the contest: rally, figure (driving skills), and maintenance. He performed well in the contest, but ultimately finished second. In the rally, he completed the course in the shortest time, but only won third place due to an engine stall. In his fifth year, Fukui finally got serious about writing his graduation thesis. Eyeing a potential job at an automaker, he wrote a paper on NO_x in exhaust gas.

In April 1969, Fukui was hired by Honda. He chose the company because he revered its founder, and admired the firm's involvement in the Formula 1 circuit, even though, at the time, Honda had suspended its participation. On entering the company, Fukui was assigned to the automobile R&D center in Wako, the lab of Honda R&D responsible for developing four-wheel vehicles. He was added to a newly created group for emissions research right around the time that the U.S. Congress was debating the 1970 Clean Air Act. Fukui was the youngest member of Honda's team to develop the landmark CVCC engine.

Honda made its debut in international motorcycle racing by entering the Isle of Man TT Race in 1959. Honda motorbikes performed brilliantly, its four-stroke machines winning a slew of World Grand Prix championships. But the company halted its racing activity by 1967 to concentrate on developing production vehicles for the mass market. A disappointed Fukui thought Honda should return to racing and made his complaint known to Tadashi Kume, then president of Honda R&D.

In 1978, Fukui found himself transferred to the motorcycle R&D center in Saitama prefecture outside Tokyo, and became involved in the development of engines for racing motorbikes. Honda president Kiyoshi Kawashima had declared the previous year that the firm would return to Formula 1 racing, and Fukui's team at the lab was tasked with developing new engines for Honda's racing machines.

Fukui's development team tackled the challenge under the slogan "Innovate to win." Instead of conventional circular pistons, the team adopted oval pistons to increase the number of valves for enhanced intake and exhaust efficiencies. Honda's new racing machine, the NR (New Racing) 500, powered by a newly developed 500cc, four-stroke engine, made its debut in a race held in the U.K. in 1979. But it proved to be susceptible to engine trouble, and failed to win the race. As the NR500s struggled to achieve success on the circuit, the Honda team developed a machine carrying a two-stroke engine dubbed the NS (New Sport) 500. With the NS500, Honda returned to the grand prix victory circle. The innovative NR project had been a disappointment for Fukui, but he quickly compensated for this failure with success of the NS project. Here was a man who could carry out a vision.

Honda's Offensive to Reclaim Green Leadership

After years of developing engines for racing motorbikes, Fukui was transferred to the U.S. to head Honda of America Mfg., Inc., the company's main North American manufacturing hub in Ohio. There, Fukui worked hard to expand Honda's operations in the U.S.

In 1998, Fukui returned to Japan, and became president of Honda R&D. The new post involved him in Honda's Formula 1 program, thus fulfilling one of his long-cherished dreams. But by that time, Fukui had sensed that the company's R&D operations were losing sight of Honda's true culture. He lamented that the company was just not producing cars that embodied the distinctive hallmark traits of Honda and its proud tradition of innovation.

Fukui thought Honda would go on producing colorless vehicles unless it re-energized its R&D operations. Fukui's answer to this identity crisis was a new management strategy focused on reviving Honda's original ethos and traditional culture. In pursuing this strategy, Fukui started showing up at labs frequently to have talks with researchers and other employees. He focused his efforts on fostering an atmosphere that allowed employees to do what they really wanted to.

Fukui told young employees that Honda was a company that encouraged its employees to seek and tackle challenges head-on. "Don't give up hope even if you fail badly," he would urge, drawing on his own experiences.

"Honda was not lagging behind Toyota in developing hybrid technology," Fukui recalls. "Our first hybrid model was a two-seater sports car. Toyota's Prius is a full-fledged sedan. We simply failed to match Toyota in its enthusiasm for hybrid technology."

But Fukui is not a man who concedes defeat easily. In 2006, he launched Honda on an ambitious campaign to reclaim leadership in environmental technology, and made it a pillar of his efforts to restore the company's original corporate identity.

In May 2006, Fukui announced Honda's new long-term production and development plan, which features projects to put the company back on the cutting edge of automotive innovation. "We will try to create new value through manufacturing and reinforce our foundations for growth in the world market," Fukui declared.

One of the key projects in this plan is the 2009 launch of a new model as only a hybrid, just as the Prius is available only as a hybrid. This is a tack Honda had not been keen to pursue due to its projected low profitability, until recently. The plan also calls for the rolling out of a fuel-cell vehicle.

The hybrid model will be manufactured at Honda's plant in Suzuka, Mie prefecture, and priced lower than 2.2 million yen (US$19,000), the average price tag of a Civic Hybrid—Honda's current flagship hybrid. The company hopes to sell 200,000 units of the new hybrid per year. Honda is also working on next-generation diesel-engine technology, and plans to launch within a three-year span a new four-cylinder diesel engine that emits no more NO_x than a gasoline engine. Honda has also revealed a plan to develop a V6 diesel engine. The fuel-cell vehicle, too, has a three-year window.

The new long-term business plan that Fukui and his team outlined contained some 20 investment and development projects, including the construction of three new manufacturing plants in Japan and North America. Its sales target for four-wheel vehicles was set at 4.5 million units in 2010, up 34 percent from 2005.

The ambitious plan represents a turning point for Honda management. The reform and restructuring efforts under the presidencies of Kawamoto and Yoshino allowed Honda to survive the wave of consolidation that swept through the world auto industry, and Honda did manage to emerge stronger from the shakeup. Honda concentrated on securing stable revenue flows to consolidate its competitive footing.

But this strategy came at a price. Honda lost its way. The company's traditional go-getting spirit, which characteristically united the entire workforce with a single-minded sense of purpose, shifted to a more defensive posture. Honda's new business expansion plan struck industry watchers as a positive sign that president Fukui was fully in control, and bent on redirecting the company on the path to recapture its cachet.

Committed to Hybrid Affordability

In retrospect, there had been telltale signs of a sea change at Honda. In February 2006, I visited Honda's R&D lab in a suburb of Utsunomiya, Tochigi prefecture, to find out how the company's hybrid development project was going, and was lucky enough to happen upon Fukui, who was just getting out of his car. "What are you doing here?" he queried, somewhat suspiciously. I didn't realize it at the time, but he was visiting the lab to give a pep talk to the researchers at the facility for an upcoming "clean car" offensive, which included the development of the new hybrid-only model, and was probably wondering whether this information had been leaked.

Around this time, Fukui started pressing for greater efforts to cut the manufacturing costs of hybrids. He told Honda's hybrid development team to reduce the price gap between hybrids and the corresponding gasoline vehicles to less than 200,000 yen (US$1,700).

"If the price gap is narrowed further, the popularity of hybrids will rise dramatically," he said. He also argued that hybrids were good for the health of the planet, but still far too expensive.

As a matter of fact, hybrid vehicles are considerably more expensive than gasoline-powered cars. The list price of a Prius with a 111-horsepower, hybrid power train is 2.26 million yen (US$19,700), almost US$4,000 higher than that of an Toyota Allion, a sedan powered by a 132-horsepower gasoline engine. The catalog figure for Prius gas mileage is 35.5 kilometers per liter of gasoline (83.5 miles per gallon), much better than Allion's 16.2 (38.1 miles per gallon). But one could argue the higher fuel economy doesn't make up for the huge price differential. Much the same is true for Honda's hybrid cars. The Civic Hybrid, with a power train that combines a 95-horsepower gasoline engine and a 20-horsepower electric motor, is about US$3,500 more expensive than a gasoline-powered Civic.

"What we are trying to make is a hybrid for everyone," says Toyotaka Sonoda, a senior researcher at Honda R&D, who heads the team in charge of developing the next-generation hybrid system. "We still stick to our principal project goal of achieving the best possible efficiency in both horsepower and gas mileage, but we will try to eliminate all inefficiencies to enable mass production of a hybrid on a gasoline vehicle scale."

Sonoda led Honda's project to develop its first hybrid vehicle, the Insight, from 1996–1998, paving the way for the development of Civic Hybrid. While Honda trailed Toyota in launching the first mass-market hybrid car, it improved on its system to develop hybrids for general consumers. The efforts led to the development and mass production of a 1.3-liter Civic Hybrid in 2002 and a 1.5-liter Civic Hybrid in 2005. These models established Honda as the number two hybrid maker in the world, behind Toyota.

Critical for expanding the market in hybrid vehicles are effective efforts to make hybrid systems smaller, lighter, and less expensive. Honda boosted the efficiency of the motor by changing the positioning of its magnets, and increased the output by using coils with high-density windings. The cooling system, which was previously designed to cool the battery and the inverter separately, was reduced in size, while rare metals were adopted as the motor material for higher output. "We can still cut costs substantially by taking steps like designing a more efficient structure and integrating electronic components into automotive parts," claims Sonoda, stressing that a popularly priced hybrid is something well within reach.

To its credit, Toyota is very good at cutting costs. The company has been trying to halve the costs for every hybrid model changeover. Technology is not the only factor at play. Automakers need to lower prices through manufacturing ingenuity and economies of scale, so that they can beat out their competitors in the green realm.

Sights Set on Commercially Viable Fuel-Cell Vehicles

Fukui's environmental strategy envisions a wide assortment of clean-running cars, including not just hybrids but also clean diesel cars and fuel-cell vehicles.

"The ultimate green car will be powered by a fuel cell. The technology will completely transform automobile manufacturing," asserts Fukui, who, as do many other automakers, seems especially keen on bringing fuel-cell vehicles to market.

Toyota and Honda, again, have led strong fuel-cell initiatives. In December 2002, the two companies delivered their respective fuel-cell vehicles to the prime minister's office in what has become a tradition. At the delivery ceremony, then Prime Minister Junichiro Koizumi test-drove the vehicles. A new battle had begun.

A fuel-cell vehicle is powered by electricity generated through the chemical reaction between hydrogen in a tank and oxygen taken from the air. Since a fuel-cell vehicle produces no tailpipe emissions except for water, it is often touted as the ultimate green car. Fuel-cell technology is already in practical use, as testified to by the fact that the government has decided to lease such vehicles.

But there is still a long road to travel before cars powered by a fuel cell come into widespread commercial use. The fuel-cell vehicles that have been manufactured so far are oddly shaped and prohibitively costly to build. Currently, manufacturing a fuel-cell vehicle costs 100 million yen (US$870,000). Moreover, the necessary infrastructure, including hydrogen-fueling stations, is simply not in place. There are also some technological issues to be solved. Water produced through the chemical reaction turns to ice when the temperature is low.

Fukui has, however, announced a specific timeframe for launching Honda fuel-cell vehicles. Its newest fuel-cell vehicle, which was on display at the media event in September 2006, looked much smarter than the previous model, giving off the impression that the project was approaching the commercialization stage.

Honda's FCX Concept, unveiled at the Tokyo Motor Show in October 2005, was equipped with a hydrogen tank that incorporated a specially developed hydrogen absorbent, which allowed for a doubling of the maximum amount of hydrogen that can be carried, to 5 kilograms (11 pounds), without making the tank larger. At the Detroit Auto Show in January 2006, Honda announced that its fuel-cell vehicle would soon have a travel range on a par with a gasoline-powered car. The company also demonstrated a device to allow users to fill up the hydrogen tank at home.

"Honda is leading other automakers in development of technologies needed to manufacture fuel-cell vehicles," claims Yozo Kami, a chief engineer at Honda R&D, who heads the FCX project. "In the early 2010s, fuel-cell technology will reach the end of the development phase, and enter an era of business competition over lowering cost and manufacturing large volumes. We need to bring costs down to levels that allow us to offer the vehicle at consumer-accessible prices. By improving the manufacturing process and marketing approach for high-volume sales, we will probably reach that goal around 2015."

Kami joined Honda in 1969 upon graduating from the University of Tokyo in engineering. He was involved in suspension development for the Civic and Honda Prelude before being assigned to the FCX project. In 1998, Kami was issued a mandate by then president Yoshino to "complete the fuel-cell vehicle."

"To obtain a 400-volt current, you need 400 thicknesses of electrode plates that partition the power-generation part," Kami points out. "If you make each of the plates a millimeter thinner, that will translate into a reduction in overall thickness of 400 millimeters. Through efforts to improve conductivity, such as using a metal material for the ion-exchange membrane, we can make sure that the temperature will rise more quickly, preventing the freezing of the device."

"Even if the hydrogen infrastructure for fuel-cell vehicles are not built quickly, technology to produce hydrogen from city gas would allow users to fill up the hydrogen tank at home," noted president Fukui in December 2006 when announcing a plan to start leasing new fuel-cell vehicles based on the FCX Concept.

Fukui's remarks reflected his determination to catapult Honda into the lead in the race to develop commercially viable fuel-cell cars, which many think could constitute the environmental endgame, or a very decisive battlefield. Kami is confident that his team can open up a new fuel-cell era in the automobile industry through a critical mass of improvements.

The Japanese auto industry seems to have fully embraced hybridization, which for the moment presents a more immediate approach to greener automobiles than fuel-cell technology. Although Toyota has claimed the upper hand with its hybrid system, Honda would be quick to counter that the real twenty-first-century car is yet to come.

Chapter 3

The West Strikes Back

GM, Ford Show Their Mettle

GM is by no means out of the running. The long-time undisputed leader of the auto universe may have seen hybrids as little more than a transition technology to a greener future, but knows that that future is coming.

"We face an increasingly uncertain energy future on a global basis. All this has created serious concerns about energy supply, energy availability, sustainable growth, the environment, even national security, issues that collectively have been come to be called 'energy security,'" stressed GM chairman Rick Wagoner at the 2006 Los Angeles Auto Show. "It is highly unlikely that oil alone is going to supply all of the world's rapidly growing auto-motive energy requirements. For the global auto industry... we must, as a business necessity, develop alternative sources of propulsion based on alternative sources of energy in order to meet the world's growing demand for our products. The key to all this, as we see it at GM, is energy diversity. We believe the best way to power the automobile in the years to come is to do so with many different sources of energy."

At the Detroit Auto Show the following January, Wagoner introduced his company's promising new EV concept, the

Chevrolet Volt, and underscored the importance of developing other alternative-energy solutions in the near term, such as powering vehicles with E85 ethanol—gasoline consisting of 85 percent ethanol: a renewable fuel made from corn or other starch feedstock.

The Chevrolet Volt is a plug-in hybrid. It houses a battery that can be recharged at home with an ordinary electric socket. About six hours of charging the vehicle would enable the Volt to drive a distance of about 40 miles (64.4 kilometers) before running out of juice. But when the battery runs low on energy, it could be recharged by an onboard photovoltaic engine. It would save about 500 gallons of gas a year over conventional gas cars.

The Volt is part of an initiative that Wagoner explained as an "E-flex" platform, a next-generation propulsion system that uses an electric motor to power the wheels of a vehicle, but can be configured to derive its electricity from a fuel cell, an engine, or a battery.

GM's Two-Mode Power System

In his keynote speech in Los Angeles, Wagoner had announced a commitment to signifincantly expand and accelerate development of electrically driven vehicles, characterizing plug-in hybrid systems as a "top priority." The biggest hurdle to commercialization of such vehicles, Wagoner said, lay in battery technology, and GM is currently making strides in co-developing with battery makers advanced lithium-ion batteries that could amplly power plug-in hybrid systems.

Within a matter of just six weeks, GM had unveiled at the Detroit Auto Show what seemed a very viable EV concept, but more significantly, sent a strong message to the world that it still had the technical will and wherewithal to lead the world into a brand new automotive future.

At a briefing in front of industry analysts held in a Detroit suburb during the motor show, Wagoner made clear his intention to raise as much as a billion dollars in capital in 2007 and 2008 over the amounts spent in 2006, and dispense it not only for necessary restructuring, but also for new car and technology development to maintain GM leadership in automotive design and technology.

GM had already unveiled a "two-mode" power system that uses electric power at low speeds but switches to an eight-cylinder gas-engine mode with battery assist for acceleration and climbing hills. As does the Prius, it elicits the most efficient fuel consumption and driving performance depending on driving conditions. A sophisticated electronic control system enters data on driving conditions, sets the required torque and conveys signals to the engine and electric motor. The transmission amplifies torque to generate the optimum power output, improving fuel efficiency by about 20 percent.

GM developed the core technology for the two-mode system back in the mid-1990s, in conjunction with transmission builder Allison, and had it installed in a large gas-guzzling bus, the GM Allison EP40/50 Hybrid in 2001. The system was deployed in buses in major cities throughout the country. By 2005, GM had produced about 500 of them.

"We're leveraging the same concept through our joint venture with DC [DaimlerChrysler] and BMW. If we can implement it in a diesel

Saturn Vue Green Line
Photography courtesy of © GM Corp. This image is licensed under Creative Commons 3.0 License.

car, we'll raise the clean emissions level even more," said GM Powertrain Asia Pacific manager Martin Murray.

From 2004, GM had begun installing a compact "mild" hybrid system in pickup trucks and, with battery advancements, planned to install even better fuel-efficiency hybrid systems in 2007 models of the small SUV, the Saturn Vue Green Line. What makes the GM hybrid system so remarkable is that it costs less than US$2,000 extra for the hybrid version, and gets 32 miles per gallon on the highway, the highest fuel economy for any SUV, enabling consumers to "go green without going broke."

Murray explains the GM position as "looking to respond to different consumer needs by preparing a variety of fuel-efficient options over a wide range of price points, from passenger cars to full-size SUVs."

Indeed, GM's environmental strategy is marked by its diversity. Vice president of R&D and strategic planning, Larry Burns, has stated positively that hybrids are a "transition" from the internal combustion engine to "viable alternatives," such as fuel cell and electric vehicles. He is quick to point out that hybrid car needs in Japan differ from those in the U.S., where people do a lot more freeway driving.

GM believes it has the competitive and technical strengths to develop its own hybrids and release them in accordance with market trends. That means it intends to match efforts like the Prius, if that's what consumers want. But if the goal is to achieve zero emissions, then fuel-cell development seems to harbor the greatest promise.

Ford Takes a Magnified View of Ethanol

Ford has plans of its own for leadership in the twenty-first century. Chairman William Clay "Bill" Ford Jr., the great-grandson of company founder, Henry Ford (1863–1947), took center stage at Detroit Auto Show's Cobo Center to proclaim that Ford, in 2007, would once again become a "global powerhouse." He then relinquished the floor to new president and CEO Alan Mulally—recruited from Boeing—and executive vice president Mark Fields. Mulally unveiled the new Ford Airstream, a gleaming, silver bullet-like plug-in hydrogen hybrid concept named for the luxury RV brand

Ford Airsteam Concept
Photograph sourced from public domain.

with which Ford partnered. The Airstream has a fuel cell as an onboard charger, and operates under electric power at all times.

As does GM, Ford views the clean automotive technology landscape as rich in promising choices. The company that parented the modern auto industry in 1908 with its Model T has determined to keep its options open, giving a serious look to both ethanol and plug-in hybrid solutions while trying to compete head-to-head with Toyota and Honda in the hybrid-electric space.

Beginning in 2004, Ford wasn't shy about buying key hybrid system components such as transmissions from Toyota and electric components from Toyota subsidiary Aisin AW. Very soon, Ford had started production on the Escape Hybrid at its plant in Kansas City, Missouri, touting it as the world's first "hybrid SUV." And in 2005, the Big Three automaker had already begun production on a second hybrid car, the "Mercury Mariner Hybrid." By 2006, Ford was the only American automaker with production hybrids among the top ten best sellers. All the rest were Toyota or Honda, but the Ford Escape and Mercury Mariner hybrids held the fifth and eighth spots.

Mercury Mariner Hybrid
Photograph sourced from public domain.

"We plan to expand hybrid vehicle production to 250,000 units a year," Ford Jr. exclaimed as he listed concrete numerical targets in September 2005, and announced his hybrid-centric clean-car strategy. He also projected that by 2008 Ford would have three more hybrid models out in the Ford Fusion, Mercury Milan, and Mazda Tribute Hybrid SUV, raising hybrid production tenfold from 2005, and proving that Ford meant business when it came to putting alternative-drive vehicles on the road.

Mazda Tribute Hybrid
Photography courtesy of Mazda Motor Corporation.

Ford executives looked to emphasize the Escape's success as a ringing endorsement by consumers of their bold environmental policies, and were quick to point out that hybrids are not the exclusive territory of Japanese automakers. U.S. auto manufacturers should have confidence in their own hybrids, went the message. In 2006, Ford affiliate Mazda also delivered its first hybrid car, the Mazda Tribute, to California fire departments.

Ford also began production of its 2006 model Ford F150, a pickup truck powered by ethanol, and badged as an FFV, a "flexible fuel vehicle". Consumers can choose to run regular gasoline or E85, with no difference in power. Since 1996, Ford has sold more than 1.6 million vehicles running on ethanol. The FFV F-150 joins flexible-fuel versions of the Crown Victoria, Grand Marquis, and the luxury Lincoln Town Car.

Ethanol is primarily made from corn grown across the U.S., and is cheaper than ordinary unleaded gasoline. It was singled out as a promising alternative fuel by the Bush administration, which is backing its expanded production. Already, some five million FFV vehicles ply America's roads on ethanol, but now Ford is working with ethanol producers to increase the number of fueling stations that carry it. The drawbacks of corn-based ethanol are discussed later.

Returning to fuel-cell technology, the Ford Airstream houses a lithium-ion battery that can power the vehicle for 25 miles on one charge, and cruise another 280 miles off its fuel cell. With fuel cells being positioned as the ultimate alternative energy solution for automobiles, Ford initiated a program to provide five major U.S. cities with 30 hydrogen fuel-cell vehicles, and donated five Ford Focus fuel-cell hybrids to the city of Sacramento, California, for testing.

The importance of a long-term environmental strategy was spelled out in a "sustainability report" that Ford believes, if carried out effectively, will see Ford add another hundred years to its illustrious history. The company even changed the name of its corporate citizenship report to sustainability report to better reflect the business case behind its approach to environmental and social issues.

Whenever I attend the Detroit Auto Show, I make it a point to stay at the Dearborn Inn, a 23-acre Georgia colonial retreat built in 1931 as Henry Ford's guesthouse, and a short walk from the Henry Ford Museum. There is a bus that shuttles people to the first Ford factory, The Rouge.

With its vast collection of Henry Ford memorabilia, the museum offers visitors a rich lesson in U.S. automotive history. It displays a 1906 Ford Model N Roadster, which became the precursor to the "people's car," the 1908 Model T. But also on display in one corner of the hall is an electric car developed by the Baker Motor Vehicle Company, touted in a 1910 ad as "the ideal car for town and suburban service."

A century ago, the automobile industry looked a lot like the one shaping up today, in terms of power-train diversity. There were gasoline-powered cars, steam-powered cars, and electric-powered cars all jostling for influence in a process of natural selection before the gasoline car claimed victory. History seems to be repeating itself right at the outset of another automotive century.

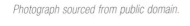

1908 Baker Electric Car
Photograph sourced from public domain.

While Ford's Model T was flying off the production line in every color as long as it was black, an industrialist named William Durant was busy snapping up every other auto company left in its wake. The result was GM. By 1927, GM was the nation's number one automaker, with a profusion of models in production.

Nearly a century later, Toyota is bidding to pass both U.S. giants to become the world's biggest auto company. Although the Prius does not figure as the main contributor to this feat, the return to century-old ideas and solutions does raise the question: what would the world look like today if we'd followed one of the other trajectories early in the twentieth century? Perhaps we are about to find out.

Daimler's Diesel Response

European makers, meanwhile, have been looking to counter the hybrid offensive by Toyota and Honda with state-of-the-art diesel technology. And Daimler has to be considered the figurehead of this effort.

Diesel cars offer greater fuel efficiency than gasoline cars, and as a result produce fewer CO_2 emissions. But they also emit more diesel particulate matter (PM) into the air through a blackish tailpipe exhaust, which has traditionally turned off American and Japanese consumers. But European automakers have been making significant strides to reduce PM since the latter half of the 1990s. Both Japan and the U.S. continue to enforce strict regulations on diesel fuel, but Daimler has great confidence in its technological might, and sees immense opportunity in a full-scale deployment of newer, cleaner-running diesel cars into what have largely been untapped markets for those products.

New Diesel Engines Pry Open Japanese-U.S. Markets

"In a highly competitive global market, appealing to the user means producing engines that are economical and clean. We have the solution with the world's best fuel efficiency and environmental performance diesel engine, BlueTec."

Mercedes E320CDI
Photography courtesy of Daimler AG.

DaimlerChrysler CEO Dieter Zetsche, with his flair for showmanship and thick handlebar mustache, waved his arms aloft at the 2006 Detroit Auto Show as he extolled the virtues of the next-generation diesel engine. Zetsche, who had taken over the helm from Jurgen Schrempp—the architect of the 1998 merger between Daimler-Benz and Chrysler—and the man credited for turning Chrysler around and putting it back on track, was setting his sights on hitting the U.S. and Japanese markets with a new-model diesel car.

Starting in Japan, in August 2006, DaimlerChrysler had begun selling an E-Class Mercedes-Benz, the E320 CDI Avantgarde, housing a cutting-edge three-liter, V6 diesel engine priced at 8.4 million yen (US$68,000), and had been doing so ahead of the diesel passenger car's full-fledged entry into U.S. and Japanese markets. "Green and powerful, it is the most efficient diesel car ever" glowed DaimlerChrysler Japan's president and CEO, Hans Tempel, referring to the car's fuel economy rating, which, at a 11-12 kilometers per liter, achieved 20-30 percent greater fuel efficiency than a gasoline version, E380, of the same class.

The decisive factor behind its high fuel efficiency was the "common rail direct injection" (CDI) technology that Daimler-Benz had co-developed with German automotive component maker Robert Bosch GmbH, specifically for diesel engines. The primary feature was its high-voltage, precision fuel-injection controls, achieving vast improvements in tailpipe emissions and noise—the traditional Achilles' heel of diesel engines. The archetype for that technology had long been developed in Japan, but had not been rolled out. But Bosch improved the technology to suit European driving, greatly contributing to the spread of diesel cars in European markets.

Bosch was aggressive about selling its diesel engine in Japan, and held a "Clean Diesel Autumn Fiesta 2006" in Tokyo's busy Shibuya district to showcase this latest technology as the one that would transform the image of diesel as clean, powerful, and economical.

Indeed, diesel-powered cars had grown in number across the then fifteen countries of the European Union (EU). In 1991, they accounted for about 20 percent of all new vehicles sold. By 2005, that figure had swollen to 49 percent, with France being the biggest diesel buyer, at 69 percent of all new vehicles sold.

Relying on diesel as its main technology, Daimler offers diesel engines in every model and class of car it sells in Europe. In total, 54 percent of new Mercedes-Benz models house diesel engines.

Daimler engines are 10 percent more economical than conventional diesel engines to run, bolstering driving performance, and boost acceleration speed and maneuverability. They also meet the stringent EU4 standards without the need for a diesel particulate filter. Daimler plans in the future to add so-called biofuels to its diesel system, combining a variety of techniques and filters to diesel hybrid vehicles.

Sensors made by Japanese pressure gauge-manufacturing giant, Nagano Keiki Co., have played a big part in the development of the common rail fuel injection device that has so greatly contributed to diesel car popularity in Europe. Bosch actually continued to use Nagano Keiki products until it could start producing sensors on its own. Nagano Keiki president Shigeru Miyashita sanguinely noted that if diesel engine vehicles finally make inroads into Japan, there will certainly be an immense role for his company to play.

The Japanese government, however, has incrementally tightened regulations on the emissions that diesel engines produce. New long-term restrictions came into force in October 2005, and there are plans to introduce more restrictions, with the aim of reducing NO_x and PM levels to zero.

Meanwhile, the EU has mandated that automakers selling vehicles inside the region's borders cut CO_2 emissions by 35 percent, to 1995 levels, by 2012, putting increasing pressure on automakers to keep pushing clean-technology innovation, in whatever form that may assume.

Refining BlueTec

The BlueTec technology that Daimler president, Zetsche, announced with great fanfare is primarily an NO_x reduction system. But since it works to reduce all components of diesel emissions, it can meet U.S. and Japanese emissions standards, and achieve 20 percent to 40 percent gains in fuel efficiency over conventional gasoline engines.

Zetsche was on hand at the Tokyo Motor Show in October 2005 to demonstrate the advantages of BlueTec. He was a big draw at the show, having just been named DaimlerChrysler president at the time. But at one point, Zetsche abruptly sat down and began playing a Bach piece on the violin with members of his booth. "The first violin is the cornerstone of an orchestra. But it's also a member of a team," Zetsche said afterward. "I believe in the principle that a great car is created as great music—through discipline, team work and harmony."

Zetsche again highlighted the advantages of BlueTec at the 2006 and 2007 motor shows in Detroit, hyping diesel as ready to run alongside other clean-running cars. He later invited the throng of automotive journalists on hand to continue the discussion over at the "Firehouse," where they could talk all night. The Firehouse is an actual firehouse located across the street from Detroit's Cobo Center. Each year, Chrysler rents it, and turns it into a beer garden for customers. Zetsche himself has been known to serve as bartender.

Daimler installed BlueTec technology in its 2007 Mercedes-Benz E320 for a release in the U.S. in 2007 and Europe in 2008. With the claim that it can enable a car to go 100 kilometers (62 miles) on 6.7 liters (1.7 gallons) of fuel, it may prove a technology to be reckoned with.

But Daimler's clean-car strategy, naturally, doesn't end with diesel. When Daimler was still DaimlerChrysler, Dr. Thomas Weber, deputy member of the board in charge of research and technology, painted the company's future energy strategy as occurring over five stages. The first calls for optimization of the internal combustion engine, followed by improvement of conventional fuels. Third is biofuel, with hybrids representing the fourth step, and fuel cells as the fifth. Other German automakers, such as VW and BMW, share the emphasis on making internal combustion engines more efficient.

DaimlerChrysler had formed a coalition with GM and BMW to pool research resources, and save on costs for next-generation hybrid development. The three companies assembled a total of 400 engineers in the city of Troy, outside Detroit, to take part in joint development of everything from so-called "mild" to "full" hybrid technologies. The venture has already generated promising results, as was in evidence at the 2006 Detroit Auto Show, when the two-mode drive was unveiled as "the hybrid system of the future."

The World Leans Toward Diesel

DaimlerChrysler Japan CEO, Hans Tempel, was in attendance at a breakfast sponsored by the Institute for New Era Strategy, chaired by Tetsuo Kondo, a former Labor minister and director of Japan's Economic Planning Agency. The theme of the meeting was

"Hybrid versus Diesel—Japan and Germany's automotive environmental strategies."

Tempel contended that ever since the development of the common rail fuel injection system, diesel engines had witnessed dramatic improvements, leading to highly reliable, economical, and remarkably high-performance vehicles.

Also present at the meeting was Toyota executive technical advisor Hiroyuki Watanabe, who quickly concurred. "Toyota has been looking hard at fuel-efficient diesel technology, and is making efforts to develop clean diesel concurrent with hybrids." Watanabe then added, "I don't see Japanese and German green strategies as 'hybrid vs. diesel,' but as 'hybrid and diesel.'"

Toyota's own clean diesel technology, to which Watanabe had alluded, is referred to as the "Toyota D-CAT System." As does the common rail system, it uses high-precision fuel-injection controls to reduce greatly, and simultaneously, both NO_x and PM through Toyota's highly touted DPNR catalyst system.

European regulations for NO_x are 0.25 grams per kilometer (g/km; 0.006 ounces per mile) but the D-CAT system weighs in within the 0.15 to 0.20 g/km range. Furthermore, there is data suggesting a further improvement to 0.05 g/km (0.001 ounces per mile). The D-CAT system is already installed in the Toyota Avensis diesel, and is being sold in European markets.

European sales of Japanese-made diesel cars have risen dramatically in recent years. Approximately 25 percent of all Japanese cars sold in the EU in 2005 were diesel. Although European makers also provide diesel engines, most Japanese diesel vehicles now employ Japanese diesel-engine technology. Against the background of increasing pressure for cleaner cars and reducing costs, Japanese makers are beginning to see great benefits in diesel-engine development.

Margo Oge, director of the EPA's Office of Transportation and Air Quality, cited report findings that "if one-third of all light-duty trucks in the U.S. were operated with modern diesel engines, the country would save 1.4 million barrels of oil per day." This is equivalent to the amount of oil the U.S. currently imports from Saudi Arabia.

The History of the Diesel Engine

The internal combustion engine essentially began with a German man named Nikolaus Otto in 1876. Otto built what would be the origin of the modern gasoline engine, a four-cycle device that uses spark ignition to get one combustion per two revolutions. Another German inventor, Gottlieb Daimler, in 1883 refined it into a smaller, more lightweight, and practical four-cycle engine, and in 1886 installed it in two-wheeled and four-wheeled vehicles. That year, Karl Benz acquired a patent for a gasoline engine-powered vehicle, and put an electric-ignition, four-cycle engine into a three-wheeled vehicle. The gasoline engine, in comparison with the steam engine used to date, was lighter, more compact, and capable of generating more output, making it perfectly suited as an internal combustion, locomotive drive for the automobile. Thus the age of the gasoline-powered automobile began.

The diesel engine was developed not long after the gasoline engine in 1892 with an "internal combustion locomotive process and application" patent acquired by German engineer Rudolf Diesel. The basic principle was that when extreme pressure is applied, temperature in the internal combustion rises, and can be used to ignite the fuel.

The greatest difference between the gasoline and diesel engines lies in the method of burning fuel, combustion. The gasoline engine pushes a mixture of air and gasoline into the cylinder, which is burned by the ignition of a spark plug. Gasoline combustion and ignition are its hallmark traits. By contrast, the diesel engine compresses the air that is sucked up into the cylinder. When that pressurized air becomes very hot, fuel is injected into the cylinder as atomized particles, and fuel consumption takes place by self-lighting. Light oil fuel and self-ignition are its main traits.

With the diesel engine, a carburetor is used to mix a fine spray of liquid fuel in advance, and the throttle is used to control output. As a fuel-injection system, a fuel pump and injector are needed. For this reason, it has a more complicated structure than a gasoline engine. But with the pressure ratio high, a diesel engine can generate higher torque and leaner combustion, resulting in higher fuel efficiency than that of the gasoline engine and fewer CO_2 emissions. The drawback, however, is that it emits more PM and considerably more NO_x into the atmosphere.

Diesel believed that he could build an engine that was far more thermally efficient than other propulsion-based internal combustion engines. And in 1897, at the University of Munich, he got his first diesel engine to work. He showed it at the Paris Expo in 1900. Interestingly, the fuel he used to power the diesel was peanut oil, making it the original biodiesel engine as well.

This prototype engine fell short of the targeted 30 percent thermal efficiency, at 26.2 percent. But at the time, it was the most fuel-efficient internal combustion device available. Of the energy required to move a steam engine at the time, no more than 10 percent of the energy generated could be used at any given time. The remainder was released into the air as heat. It was also a colossal, complex structure, which weighed 4.5 tons, so its use was limited to powering trains and boats.

In 1909, a young Lebanese engineer named Prosper L'Orange succeeded in inventing an advanced combustion-chamber fuel-injection system, followed by a funnel-type advanced combustion-chamber method and needle-injection nozzle, and an adjustable fuel-injection pump to streamline the entire structure. This opened the door to using diesel engines in automobiles.

Diesel, however, mysteriously committed suicide in 1913. He threw himself from a steam ship while crossing from Antwerp, in Belgium, to Harwich, England. A note he had written just beore his death read: "I'm confident the diesel engine for the automobile will eventually emerge. And then for the first time, my life's work will have been completed."

First Trucks, Then Automobiles

Because the diesel engine is very thermally efficient, and leads to lean fuel combustion, the problem of engine knocking, or pinging, found in internal combustion engines, caused by pockets of air/fuel mixture exploding, is also largely avoided. For this and other reasons, Benz & Company, based in Mannheim, began practical development of the diesel engine, mainly for use in large trucks for long-distance travel. In 1923, Benz became the world's first diesel-truck manufacturer with the 5K3. This was mimicked by Daimler-Motoren-Gesellschaft (DMG) and Machinery Augsburg-Nuremberg (MAN) with their own diesel vehicles, and a market for the commercial diesel vehicle was born. In the U.S., in 1929, the Packard Motor Car Company became the first to launch a diesel vehicle in that country, using a diesel engine manufactured by Cummings Co.

Mercedes-Benz 180D taxi
Photography courtesy of Daimler AG.

A very robust engine block is required to endure the high-pressure ratio of a diesel engine, which makes the engine structure more complex than that of a gasoline engine. Producing diesel engines small enough for passenger cars, therefore, is a challenge. But in 1933, Daimler-Benz unveiled a high-speed engine prototype for passenger vehicles, and then in November 1934, successfully tested the world's first passenger-car diesel engine at its Gaggenau factory. In February 1936, the world's first mass-production diesel-engine passenger car, the Mercedes-Benz 260D, was released. But although it surpassed the gasoline car in terms of fuel efficiency performance, it fell far short in terms of power, and failed to take hold in the market.

Mercedes-Benz 200D
Photography courtesy of Daimler AG.

After World War II, Mercedes-Benz resumed work on improving the diesel engine, leading to the 170D, produced at the Sindelfingen factory. It represented a significant improvement over its pre-war predecessor, the 260D, and outsold it in four years by twelve times, selling 25,000 units. Furthermore, in 1952, a four-cylinder diesel engine was installed in the 170DS to great success. That was followed by debuts of the three-box bodied, 180D and 190D in 1953. Throughout the 1950s, the Mercedes-Benz 180D became known as "the German taxi" due to its adoption by a taxi company.

The diesel engine underwent rapid improvement in performance and was deployed in a host of models including the classic "tail-fin" model, the Mercedes-Benz 200D. In 1971, diesel passenger-car production reached a grand total of a million vehicles in the post-war period.

Oil Crisis a Boon for Sales But...

Throughout the 1970s into the 1980s, diesel passenger-car sales climbed through the roof due to diesel's relative fuel efficiency during the oil crises. Sales of diesel passenger cars in the U.S. in 1981 reached an all-time high.

Although only 10 percent of GM's vehicles sold in the U.S. were diesel, 78 percent of Mercedes-Benz vehicles were of the diesel variety. Daimler-Benz then launched a brand new model, the 190, in 1982, based on the popular C Series, and then a new-model, two-liter diesel 190D in 1983. It was light, economical, and powerful, harboring a maximum 75-horsepower engine, which was completely sealed off to reduce engine noise by 50 percent. The automotive world's reaction was that this was too quiet to be a diesel.

In Japan, Toyota's 1957 Crown Diesel earned the proud distinction of being the first domestically produced diesel passenger car in Japan. But production was halted after only a few years. Later, Izusu Motors came out with a diesel passenger car in 1962, which was primarily adopted as a taxi. This diesel drove like a gasoline car, plus it had the fuel economy of a diesel, and could've supplanted the liquid petroleum gas car, which had been predominant for taxis and small trucks in Japan in the 1960s. But beginning in the latter half of the 1970s, fuel-efficient diesel passenger cars received a second look, and the number of diesel owners in Japan began to grow.

When the oil crisis of the 1970s receded, and gasoline prices dropped again, diesel cars in both Japan and the U.S. fell out of public favor, due largely to the black exhaust and particulates they spewed. With stricter emissions standards being enacted, diesel sales plummeted in the U.S., and GM eventually decided to stop production of diesel engines altogether.

In Japan, until the 1990s, environmental regulations put a priority on reduction of NO_x emissions. PM regulations, on the other hand, were more lax than those in Europe, and the sight of diesel trucks disgorging black smoke as they drove by was disturbing to the public. Tokyo governor Shintaro Ishihara was prompted

First-generation Mitsubishi Pajero
Photograph sourced from public domain.

to stage a "No to Diesel" campaign with slogans such as "We will not ride on diesel, buy diesel, or sell diesel in Tokyo." Then automobile tax reform in 1990 increased the taxation on two-liter or higher diesel-engine vehicles. An increase in the "light oil trading tax" in 1993 and the abolition of a special petroleum product import provisional measures law shrank the price differential between gasoline and light oil to a nominal amount, making gas cars nearly as economical as diesel.

Diesel saw a brief resurgence when an RV boom, sparked largely by Mitsubishi Motors' popular four-wheel-drive, turbocharged Pajero (Montero) in 1995, boosted diesel ownership to record highs for Japan. Diesel sales peaked that year, but haven't risen since.

Common Rail in Europe Lifts Diesel

Europeans view diesel differently. The diesel passenger car is increasingly being favored as a high-performance, fuel-efficient automotive choice. Europeans on average log many more kilometers than Japanese drivers over the course of a year, and are consequently more able to see the cost benefits to driving diesel cars. The percentage of diesels among all newly registered vehicles was about 15 percent in 1990, but rose to 22.3 percent by 1994, a mere four years.

Part of this is due to companies like Daimler-Benz, which took its new DPF (diesel particulate filter) technology, and deployed it for the first time in mass-production vehicles that were clean enough to be shipped and sold in California, which has some of the most stringent emissions standards anywhere in the world. Beginning in 1991, all Mercedes-Benz diesel models were fitted with emissions-recirculation devices and diesel catalytic converters.

A turning point contributing to the spread of the diesel throughout Europe came in 1997 when major auto component maker Bosch and Daimler-Benz joined forces to co-develop new diesel technologies, most notably the CDI system described earlier.

With the common-rail development greatly adding to diesel-engine performance as well as quieter operation, reduced emissions, and better fuel economy, diesel passenger cars in Europe began achieving 20 percent, or better, more fuel efficiency than standard gasoline cars, making them a much more immediate choice for individual

Mazda Atenza
Photography courtesy of Mazda Motor Corporation.

consumers wishing to take a more active role in fighting global warming. As a result, newly registered diesel cars, from the second half of the 1990s, grew by an annual 4 percent. Diesel growth in countries such as France, Belgium, and Austria exceeded 60 percent, and recently that rate has climbed to nearly 50 percent on a pan-European average.

Japanese automakers, too, have begun launching advanced diesel passenger cars such as the British-built Toyota Avensis, Honda Accord, and Mazda Atenza (Mazda 6), which won second place in the European Car of the Year in 2003. Isuzu Motors, which operates an engine factory in Poland, has begun supplying its engines in "original equipment manufacturer" style to other makers, including GM. The Toyota group is expected to roll out a wide variety of diesel technologies in the coming years, mostly aimed at Europe, through its 2006 capital tie-up with Isuzu and subsidiary truck manufacturer Hino.

In April 2005, a committee to study the dissemination and future of diesel passenger cars, formed under METI, spelled out the merits of diesel in the hopes of eliciting public re-evaluation of the technology.

"The diesel passenger cars that are currently being sold in Japan boast a level of sophistication vastly different from that of older-generation diesels. They used to be noisy, vibrate a lot, accelerate poorly, lack power, belch dirty emissions, and, on top of it all, smelled bad," noted a committee member.

In truth, Japanese users haven't been given very many opportunities to experience the new technological revolution in diesel, and diesel penetration in the market remains low. But if European automakers and even domestic players such as Honda and Toyota get their ongoing projects production ready, the diesel's time may finally arrive.

BMW Opts for Hydrogen

Although diesel remains the popular choice for improving emissions in Europe, another German auto company, BMW, is banking on hydrogen technology. The problem is cost. A single vehicle sells for about US$1 million, far out of mass-production reach. But the BMW hydrogen vehicle can also run on gasoline, and still manages to emit only water, bringing production costs to a relatively low level, while maintaining the appeal of a clean car.

From March 2007, BMW began selling its 7 Series-based hydrogen vehicle, the "Hydrogen 7," in Europe, and was set to debut in Japan in the summer of 2007. BMW expects to be able to issue a hundred vehicles in Europe, the U.S., and Asia for six-month leases.

Mazda is also in the practical development stages of a hydrogen-gas combination. Rather than liquid hydrogen, however, the vehicle is fueled by hydrogen gas, but can only run about half as long as the BMW version. The drawback for liquid hydrogen is that it must be kept at an extremely low temperature, and would take up luggage compartment space. BMW has a plan to provide hydrogen-refilling vehicles in major markets such as Japan, where they are almost nonexistent.

As a luxury-car maker, BMW still has a stake in sticking with the gasoline engine. It set up its first auto plant 111 years ago in the central German city of Eisenach. During 2002–06, its chairman of the board was a former nuclear engineer and physics professor, Helmut Panke.

Coming from a science background, Panke confessed to me in an interview that he didn't view hybrid systems as constituting a real technological advance. They simply add another two to three hundred kilograms of weight to a car.

The marketing-research firm J.D. Power and Associates projects that hybrids will never account for more than 5 percent of the total market. What seemed more important to Panke in the immediate term was improving the internal combustion engine to reduce fuel consumption. "At BMW, we currently have the technology to reduce fuel consumption by 15 percent in our three-liter, six-cylinder engines. Plus we're dedicating a lot more of our research budget to hydrogen-vehicle technology that will ensure customers are getting the kind of satisfying driving experience they've come to expect from BMW."

BMW has always managed to succeed with its own premium strategy, and isn't looking to emulate others in the environmental battle either.

Renault–Nissan Weighs Options

The Renault–Nissan alliance, headed by Carlos Ghosn, is also looking to implement a flexible clean-car strategy that doesn't rely too heavily on either hybrid or diesel. Among the "Commitments 2009" that Ghosn announced for Renault in February 2006, was a clean-car strategy to be single-mindedly carried out by Nissan and Renault together, which essentially divides the workload among them by category. Renault will handle diesel engines, Nissan will grapple with fuel cells and hybrids. Renault will foray into ethanol and manual transmissions, while Nissan develops Continuously Variable Transmission (CVT). But Ghosn reserves his highest expectations in the environmental technology realm for Nissan, which can tap deep reserves of technical know-how.

On December 11, 2006, Nissan chief operating officer Toshiyuki Shiga announced a brand new mid-term environmental action plan called "Nissan Green Program 2010," which specifically articulates a wide range of tasks and objectives, ranging from the rollout of environmentally friendly vehicles to greener factories.

"The Nissan Green Program 2010 provides a transparent view of Nissan's future commitments to all aspects of environmental management," said Shiga. "Nissan Green Program 2010 has been designed to address immediate challenges, as well as creating the foundation toward a long-term sustainable business model."

The ambitious plan, set for 2010, aims to develop Nissan's own hybrid car, continue boosting gasoline engine fuel efficiency, develop gasoline engine vehicles that can achieve the same low levels of CO_2 emissions as diesel engines or hybrid systems, and develop new clean-running diesel-engine, fuel-cell, and ethanol-based cars, as well as production EVs.

Nissan was initially hesitant to throw its resources into hybrid-car development for financial reasons. Although Nissan did start selling a hybrid vehicle in the U.S. in 2007, it did so with licensing help from Toyota. Nissan began selling a hybrid version of its breadwinning sedan, Altima. But upon seeing the aggressive response by North American and European automakers to cut into the hybrid action, Nissan altered its policy, and decided to develop its own hybrid for sales in Japan and North America.

Nissan Altima Hybrid
Photography courtesy of Nissan Motor Co., Ltd.

In addition, Nissan planned to unveil a new-model, two-liter diesel vehicle in Europe in 2007, along with plans to build a diesel car by 2010 that can clear emission standards in the U.S., Japan, and China.

But Ghosn is also bullish about making landmark improvements to the gasoline car. His strategy calls for rolling out a seven-speed, automatic-transmission vehicle in 2007, selling a million CVT vehicles per year, adopting direct injection and next-generation turbo engine technologies, and fuel-efficient cars that reduce fuel consumption and CO_2 emissions by 20 percent, starting fiscal 2010.

One of the principal objectives of the strategy is to release in Japan, by 2010, a "three-liter car" that combines a CVT and the ability to travel 100 kilometers on three liters of gasoline (or 62.1 miles on less than a gallon of gas). If fuel efficiency in a regular gasoline car can be ramped up from an average 15 kilometers per liter (35.28 miles per gallon) to an average 33 kilometers per liter (77.62 miles per gallon) in this three-liter car, it will set a new standard for fuel economy among conventional gas automobiles.

In addition, Nissan plans to release a 100-percent ethanol-powered car in Brazil by 2010, a new model fuel-cell vehicle to come out after 2010, and an EV in the first half of the second decade. To that end, the plan also discusses production and the establishment of a sales company for lithium-ion batteries for use in hybrids and EVs.

"We will raise the level of fuel efficiency across all Nissan vehicles through a broad application of environmental technologies," said Shiga. Together with reducing CO_2 emissions in all its factories to 7 percent below 2005 levels, the concrete action plan is as ambitious about green assembly as it is about automobiles. Nissan plans to expand its use of co-generation systems, which capture heat produced when generating electricity, raise overall energy efficiency, and contribute to reduced CO_2 emissions. Nissan also seeks to make greater use of natural energy sources, such as wind and solar power, in their plants. In logistics, the company is promoting a "modal shift" in transport methods toward railway use, which has a lesser environmental load, and is examining ways to share shipping methods with Renault. On a global scale, the plan calls for measuring CO_2 emissions from 2006 to serve as a benchmark for reducing emissions in 2007.

Keeping a Wide-Ranging Research Portfolio

"At this point, we really don't know what environmental technology is going to win out, so there's a need to explore the potential of them all," remarked Ghosn during the inauguration of a global design center in the city of Atsugi, Kanagawa prefecture, only one day after Shiga announced the Green Program 2010.

The Nissan Design Centre was built as a place for product planners and component makers to congregate in one location so they can coordinate design work and shorten development times. Nissan's design bases in Japan, the U.S., U.K., and Taiwan play a large role in producing best-selling models for Nissan. At the event, Ghosn announced a mid-term plan, to begin in 2008, aimed at boosting North American production capability, including new plant construction.

As far back as 1995, Nissan entered into an agreement with Hitachi to develop EVs, leading to the 2000 release of the Nissan Hyper Mini, which is powered by a lithium-ion battery developed by Hitachi. Then in 2000, Nissan developed its own lithium-ion battery-powered hybrid system called the "Neo Hybrid," and began marketing it as the Tino Hybrid, putting Nissan on track to compete with Honda and Toyota.

Back in 1999, when Renault purchased a large stake in Nissan, the focus for resuscitating the beleaguered Japanese giant was on selection and concentration of resources, effectively putting a freeze on the hybrid-development program. Development costs had been rising, while the rate of application was low. Ghosn therefore chose to license the THS.

Nissan Hyper Mini
Photography courtesy of Nissan Motor Co., Ltd.

Although Toyota's system differs from that of Nissan, including the use of a NiMH battery as its power source, licensing enabled Nissan to take a step forward with a hybrid system program without overtaxing its development budget. As with other automakers that got caught in the tailwinds of Toyota and Honda's hybrid drive, Nissan may ultimately choose to go a different route. In

2001, Renault and Nissan together allocated about 85 billion yen for a joint fuel-cell vehicle project.

Nissan's Revival

Renault and Nissan entered into a capital alliance on March 27, 1999, in which Renault took a controlling 36.8 percent equity stake in the once proud Japanese giant. After sealing the agreement at Nissan headquarters in Tokyo, Renault chairman Louis Schweitzer and Nissan president Yoshikazu Hanawa dined on sushi, wine, and pleasant conversation before going to meet with the press at the *Keidanren* (Japan Federation of Economic Organizations). There, they announced their plans to share production platforms, sales and production networks, procurement, and a host of other synergies they hoped to reap from the historic union. Ghosn would be sent to Nissan as its chief operating officer, along with three other Renault executives, and Nissan would also reciprocate by sending executives to Renault. Although Renault would in effect run Nissan, Schweitzer made it a point to say the partnership would be one of mutual learning among equals.

Renault, founded by three brothers who began building automobiles in 1898 in the Paris suburb of Boulogne-Billancourt, was nationalized after World War II, giving the company's products the label of a "public servant's car." After the oil crises in the 1970s, it became evident that the company's weak constitution wouldn't survive the stiff global competition that lay ahead, and the French government privatized the company again.

Schweitzer, who had worked in the finance ministry, then stepped in as the company's president in 1990, and became its chairman in 1992, promoting "growth, expansion, and globalization" as its objectives. In 1996, as part of this globalization strategy, Schweitzer recruited Ghosn away from French tire giant Michelin S.A., where he was serving as president of the North American division, and assigned him the post of senior vice president. Schweitzer had been very keen on making a foray into

Asian markets, and when he saw the landmark announcement in May 1998 that brought Daimler-Benz and Chrysler together, he initiated talks with Nissan, a company that despite a glorious history was on the brink of collapse.

Nissan's Rise and Demise

In 1933, around the same time the Toyota Motor Company was being founded, the Automobile Manufacturing Company (*Jidosha Seizo Kabushiki-gaisha*) was given life by a man named Yoshisuke Aikawa, head of the *zaibatsu* (conglomerate) holding company, Japan Industries (*Nippon Sangyo*). The firm was started through a joint venture with the Tobata Casting Company, and the following year in 1934, the name was shortened from *Nippon Sangyo* to Nissan. The newly minted Nissan Motor Company immediately took over manufacturing rights to a vehicle built by one of its subsidiaries, Kwaishinsha Motorcar Works, called the Datsun. Nissan built a factory in Yokohama, and began churning out passenger cars, laying the groundwork, along with Toyota, for the rise of Japan's auto industry.

Although passenger-car production was halted during World War II, and the company closed down as part of the U.S.-led allied occupation's efforts to dismantle the Japanese war machine, Nissan did find a way to survive. That was because of a man named Katsuji Kawamata, a former Hiroshima branch manager of the Japan Industrial Bank, who had assumed managing directorship at Nissan. Kawamata successfully fought back a labor-union movement that was growing powerful in the turbulence of the postwar period, by employing lockouts and deft personnel moves. In 1957, under Kawamata's stewardship Nissan, eventually struck gold with the Datsun Bluebird. The passenger-car market was burgeoning, and Nissan went on to add new models and establish a full production-line system to meet the growing demand.

Nissan ran neck and neck with Toyota throughout the 1950s and 1960s. In the 1970s, however, it started losing market share, and by 1994, was operating in the red. According to a former mid-level manager who left to join a startup, "Nissan didn't have products that consumers wanted, nor any kind of structured strategy, global or otherwise. There was nobody thinking from a companywide basis. Everything was conducted within the individual departments, even down to support for ceremonial occasions in the life of employees. No information was being exchanged between divisions."

"Nissan in 1999 was in extremely bad shape," said Ghosn, reflecting back on the atmosphere when he took over. "Anyone could have looked at the numbers and how things were run, and told you that there would be nothing left of the company if things were allowed to continue unchecked for another ten years. People didn't have a very good idea of what was happening around them. They had built walls around themselves behind which to hide. There was no vision. And without vision, there is no strategy, no priorities, no measure, even, for deciding what's important and what is not."

After his first year at the helm, Ghosn announced, in March 2000, huge deficits of 680 trillion yen (US$6 billion). But through a three-year management-restructuring plan dubbed the "Nissan Revival Plan," he closed down domestic plants, and greatly lowered the company's debt. By the end of the second year, fiscal 2001, Nissan was posting record-breaking profits of 331 trillion yen (US$3 billion), reaching the goal of returning the company to profitability one year ahead of schedule.

Of the five major reforms that Ghosn says were necessary, "management reform" was particularly important. Nissan's crisis was not an accounting crisis, but a management crisis, Ghosn stated at a March 2003 breakfast held at the Japan Center for Economic Research.

When Nissan came to Renault, and offered an equity stake in the company, the management machinery required to maintain Nissan had clearly ceased to function. Japanese banks were reeling from a financial crisis of their own, and hadn't the wherewithal to come to Nissan's aid. Nissan had no choice but to find a way out of its morass by itself. Nissan looked for outside help, and found it with Renault, and Carlos Ghosn.

The Ghosn Reforms

The first step Ghosn took was to organize internal division heads into crossfunctional teams, or CFTs. These teams would constitute the core of people to craft the Nissan Revival Plan. Workers were empowered with various roles in the revival so as to get them actively involved since many feared or doubted the ability of reforms to get them out of the crisis. Together with CFT members, they helped craft a clear vision and a reform plan that was just as much top down as it was bottom up.

Carlos Ghosn
Photography courtesy of
Nissan Motor Co., Ltd.

Ghosn's reform also included a little shock therapy. Of the 1,394 companies that Nissan held stock in, only four were seen as indispensable to Nissan's future. The plan was also to reduce the number of parts suppliers that Nissan carried from 1,145 down to less than 600 by 2002. When Ghosn announced his revival plan, it sent shock waves down the Nissan *keiretsu* chain—basically a grouping or family of affiliated companies that form a tight-knit alliance working toward mutual success. Ghosn wanted to reduce procurement costs by 20 percent in three years, signing the death warrant for any *keiretsu* affiliate that couldn't achieve that target.

"We have to escape from the burning platform," Ghosn admonished. "You can't stay calm when your house is burning down around you. Those employees without a sense of crisis need to be awakened. This is a company where market share has been declining for 26 years; a company that hasn't recorded a profit in the last seven of eight years. It's important that people realize that this can't be viewed as anything but a crisis." Ghosn needed

Nissan workers to move beyond denial for the plan to work. "After 26 years of declining market share, there was so much negativity that had permeated down to the core of the company." A change in attitude was, of course, the gateway to recovery.

"The second reason we were able to turn things around was we chose the right path. We made a strong assessment of our situation, and that led us to move in the right direction. If the first step you take is in the right direction, the strength and confidence to take the second come easier," Ghosn said when assessing the first complete year of the revival plan in November 2000 at the Foreign Correspondent's Club of Japan.

As mentioned, Ghosn succeeded in achieving the goals of his revival plan in two years, rather than the originally projected three. So for fiscal 2002, he and his team drew up another three-year plan called "Nissan 180," signaling that the company, having climbed up out of the cellar, would now turn itself around, and head upward. It raised global auto sales targets by a million vehicles, and operating margins by 8 percent. Ghosn also promised to reduce interest-bearing debt in the auto sphere to zero.

With this success, Ghosn was named CEO of Nissan, and in 2005 also became CEO for Renault. Nissan continued to increase earnings and profits. When results were announced in March 2006, Nissan posted sales of US$78 billion and operating profits of US$7.3 billion. Cost reduction efforts such as the joint procurement and platform sharing between Renault and Nissan had proven effective, allowing Nissan to invest its capital aggressively, and launch new models in North America and China.

It wasn't until the mid-year performance assessments were announced in September 2006 that Nissan had posted its first real decline in profits since the Ghosn reform era began. Nissan, then, was unable to avoid a decline in consolidated profits when the fiscal year ended in 2006. Some of the momentum had been blunted by the soaring expansion of profits being recorded by domestic rivals Toyota and Honda. Compared with Toyota and Honda, Nissan doesn't make a lot of cars popular for their fuel efficiency, and quality issues emerged regarding Nissan SUVs built in the still relatively young Canton plant in the U.S.

Suddenly, Ghosn was back in crisis mode. "Nissan faces a performance crisis," remarked Ghosn in February 2007 in response to the first drop in earnings since he took over. Ghosn continued to say that expanding the alliance would be dangerous without an improvement in performance, alluding to his intent to focus on internal improvements, not outside solutions. "We don't need a culture of excuses at Nissan," said Ghosn in a management-training video.

Ghosn was born in Brazil in March 1954. His mother was French, his father the son of a Lebanese national who emigrated to Brazil. His father worked for a domestic airline in Brazil. As soon as Ghosn was born, the family moved to Rio de Janeiro. In 1968, at 14, Carlos attended Notre Dame High School in Beirut, a Christian school, where he studied French. At 16, he went to France alone, and went on to receive an engineering degree from the prestigious École Polytechnique in 1978. Upon graduation, Ghosn was hired by Michelin, and by 1989 was president of the company's North American operations. He was credited for the successful short-term integration of U.S. tire giant Uniroyal Goodrich after it was acquired by Michelin.

Just about that time, Renault was privatizing, and was scouting for personnel for its international division. Ghosn's natural management instincts were noticed. He has come to be widely revered in Japan for not only saving a national institution in Nissan, but bringing to Japan the "cultural fusion," or "diversification," that accompanies globalization. Japanese firms looking to globalize are now treating the new corporate culture Ghosn brought to Nissan as a business model. Although there are a lot of expectations placed on this model, sustaining growth after a V-shaped recovery will likely require a new response, different from anything that has preceded it.

Comparison of "Green" Automobiles to Gasoline Automobiles

Type of car	Power source	Cost over gas car	Fuel efficiency over gasoline car	Fuel price per liter	CO$_2$ emissions	Other emissions
Gasoline	Gasoline combustion	————	————	144 regular	Yes	NO$_x$
Diesel	Light diesel oil combustion	Thousands of dollars	10–20%	122 yen (app. US$1)	Less than gasoline	NO$_x$ (more than gasoline), PM
Hybrid	Gasoline combustion + electric motor	Thousands of dollars	50%	144 regular (app. US$1.16)	Less than gasoline and diesel cars	NO$_x$ (less than gasoline and diesel)
Electric	Electric motor	NA	NA	1 yen per kilometer	None	None
Fuel cell	Electric motor (driven by hydrogen – oxygen chemical reaction)	About ten thousand dollars	NA	NA	None	Water

Source: Nibon Keizai Shimbun, November 11, 2007

Chapter 4

Other Green Alternatives

The Promise of Bioethanol

One alternative to the environmental technologies that have received extensive treatment in this book so far is ethanol. Plant-based ethanol as an energy source for automobiles has only recently begun to receive increased attention in Japan.

Ethanol is an abbreviation for ethyl alcohol, an alcoholic ingredient, which is primarily produced from sugar cane or corn. In the major sugar cane-producing country of Brazil, for example, FFVs running on a mixture of gasoline and ethanol are outpacing conventional gasoline cars in sales.

When former Japanese Prime Minister Shinzo Abe launched his new cabinet and administration in September 2006, one of his first measures was to back a plan to promote the use of ethanol fuel. The "New National Energy Strategy" that his government drafted currently has as one of its primary objectives the reduction of Japanese reliance on imported oil from about 50 percent of energy needs to less than 40 percent by 2030.

The strategy sets out, in particular, to reduce the nearly 100 percent reliance on foreign oil in the transport sector to about 80 percent dependence by 2030. With the inclusion of a plan to have the E10 ethanol–gasoline mix account for nearly 10 percent of transportation energy needs, the Japanese government has been extolling the important role that biofuels can play in diversifying the nation's energy resources and reducing oil dependence. While ethanol does emit CO_2 when burned, the plants that constitute its raw materials absorb CO_2 through photosynthesis. The amount of CO_2 being released into the environment, therefore, does not increase. You're putting back what has already been absorbed, rather than adding more CO_2 to the atmosphere.

Ethanol Gets a Test Run at the Pumps

To meet the targets for reduction of greenhouse gases that it committed to when signing the Kyoto Protocol, the Japanese government, in 2005, compiled a plan to produce the equivalent of 500,000 kiloliters (419,321 U.S. barrels) of crude oil with plant-based fuels.

Bioethanol is made by pulverizing sugar cane or corn, letting it ferment, and then distilling it. A single hectare (2.471 acres) of sugar-cane field producing 85 tons of sugar cane can yield roughly 7.04 kiloliters (1,859 gallons, or 59 barrels) of biofuel. That is the equivalent of 9.5 kiloliters (1,321 gallons or 42 U.S. barrels) of oil. Domestic field research into whether bioethanol can actually be used as automotive fuel is currently being conducted in six locations around the country, including on Miyako island in Japan's southernmost prefecture of Okinawa. In the Miyako project, a local oil-merchant company, Ryuseki Corporation, worked with the Okinawa Sugar Manufacturing Co. to complete a plant in 2006 that produces an ethanol and gasoline mixture by fermenting the molasses from the sugar-refining process. Road tests using public vehicles running on the ethanol have so far proven promising.

The Ministry of the Environment created an eco-fuel use promotion council that was composed of government members, scholars, and industrialists to examine concrete proposals for introducing biomass-based "eco-fuels" on a massive scale by the end of 2005. Although the government did succeed in hitting its stipulated target of introducing 10 million low-emission vehicles—whether electric, natural gas, or ethanol—five years ahead of schedule, it is expected that low-emission-vehicle diffusion will escalate even further with the full-scale introduction of bioethanol and biodiesel fuels.

Running a car on sugar cane- or corn-based ethanol does not require much new infrastructure. Anything up to a 3 percent mixture of ethanol in gasoline can power automobiles without any need to revamp the car's engine, while any amount above that percentage still only requires simple reforms to existing vehicles. Newly sold cars by Toyota and Honda are, in principle, all ethanol compliant.

In 2005, in response to the government's bioethanol introduction plan, the Petroleum Association of Japan hammered out a policy to begun fully fledged sales of a bioethanol-gasoline mix by 2010 using a special additive-free gasoline called ethyl tertiary butyl ether (ETBE). In contrast with directly mixing ethanol into gasoline, it precludes the need for gasoline stations to set up special pumps, reducing infrastructure costs.

ETBE is actually a byproduct of the petroleum-refinement process. It has a molecular structure similar to the methyl tertiary butyl ether (MTBE) that had been used in the U.S. as an octane-boosting gasoline additive, but had been discontinued due to its potential risks to human health and environment.

ETBE's potential has so far been borne out in Europe where it has been introduced and lauded as nontoxic. Japan's METI, with the cooperation of the petroleum industry, has therefore begun trial sales of ETBE, mixed into regular gasoline, at filling stations throughout the Tokyo metropolitan region.

Meanwhile, the Japanese Ministry of Agriculture, Forestry, and Fisheries (MAFF) is lending its support to expanded production of bioethanol from not only an environmental protection standpoint, but as part of agriculture and regional promotion policy as well. Former MAFF Minister Toshikatsu Matsuoka believed that if the demand for raw materials for bioethanol could raise agricultural production and farmer incomes, it would play a large role in much-needed regional development. He presented to the Council on Fiscal and Economic Policy a domestic production target of 6 million kiloliters (more than 5 million U.S. barrels) of bioethanol, which would equal about 10 percent of Japan's annual gasoline consumption.

Brazil Eyes Japan with Ethanol Exports

The growing attention on ethanol as an automotive-fuel alternative in other parts of the world prompted U.S. President Bush, before the midterm congressional elections in 2006, to encourage more production of corn and other crops for ethanol fuel. He went so far as to say he wanted to see ethanol production double by 2010 to 7.5 billion gallons (28.4 million kiloliters). Against rising crude-oil prices, the decision to lower reliance on Middle East oil led to the promotion of ethanol as a policy to control gasoline consumption. But the corn reserves, that would be the biggest candidate for use in ethanol fuel, have rapidly depleted, which has led to ethanol wholesale prices rising to encroach on gasoline's price, dampening the ethanol boom. Corn as a biofuel source is widely seen as a dead end. It takes too much energy to grow and harvest for the yield it offers as a fuel, and threatens to drive up food prices as more corn-fields get shifted away from food production to fuel production. It is expensive, and ends up as more of an environmental liability than a benefit. Biodiesel fuel, as was mentioned with Diesel's peanut oil, is environmentally an improvement over corn, but vegetable oils also have a low fuel yield per acre. Other more eco-friendly alternatives are still in the development phase, such as extracting ethanol from woody plants, which wouldn't affect the food chain, and might even replenish the soil. Although there is certainly a future for a whole range of biofuels to come into use, their real-world application remains a few technological leaps away.

In contrast, Brazil is riding a huge ethanol boom as the world's largest sugar-cane producer, and is expanding production with the hope of an export boost, targeting Japan. Sugar cane grows in huge amounts, and has a high yield. But it is of course limited to tropical areas. Brazil's national petroleum company, Petrobras (Petróleo Brasileiro S.A.) recently established a joint venture with the quasi-governmental, Tokyo-based industrial-alcohol manufacturer and marketer, Japan's Nippon Alcohol Hanbai Co., called the Brazil-Japan Ethanol Co., and plans to begin importing and selling industrial-use ethanol from 2007, and automotive ethanol starting in 2008. Petrobras also used its proprietary crude-oil-production technology to tap deep-sea petroleum fields, enabling Brazil to become 100 percent self-sufficient in oil, when before it had been completely reliant upon imports.

Closing in on British and Dutch multinational oil company Royal Dutch Shell as one of the world's biggest oil companies, Petrobras, as a national energy company, is on the move as a global producer and exporter of ethanol. Mitsui & Co. and other major Japanese trading companies are looking to take part in Brazil's ethanol exports.

"Brazil has entered the age of the 100 percent ethanol, flex-fuel car," said a director for the Brazilian National Agency of Petroleum, Natural Gas, and Biofuels. The country's ethanol-fuel program actually dates back to the 1973 oil crisis, when the government turned to promoting naturally made, ethanol-based fuel and sought public support for producing a mixture of bioethanol and gasoline. Initially setting the ratio range between 20 percent and 25 percent, the regulation was raised to 23 percent in 2006, then 25 percent in July 2007.

FFVs, which can run on any gas–ethanol ratio, have a good chance of stealing the eco-spotlight from hybrids and diesels, since bioethanol is a fuel that does not raise CO_2 emissions. One of the early entrants into the flex-car development race has been Italian automaker Fiat, which has a

Toyota Corolla Flex
Photograph courtesy of Toyota Motor Corp.

long history of producing cars in Brazil. But as of 2003, VW, GM, and Ford had also entered the fray. Among Japanese players, Honda began selling flex versions of its Civic and subcompact Fit models in late 2006, while Toyota began selling a flex Corolla in May 2007.

Brazilian gasoline stations have begun offering E100—100 percent ethanol—along with other mix ratios. This has given a boost to flex-car sales, with 80 percent of all new auto sales—1.1 million cars—in the first half of 2007 being of the flex variety. With new-car sales expected to grow a year-on-year 15 percent in 2007 to about 2.3 million cars, FFV sales are expected to reach the 3 million mark in less than three years.

"FFVs require some time to put together, since the parts have to be imported from Japan. But they're indispensable for competing in Brazil," says a local Honda executive. Since engines have trouble starting on ethanol on cold days, Honda added supplementary gas tanks. The Honda plant in Sao Paolo, Brazil, is producing flex cars alongside regular gas cars. Of the 65,000 or so Civic and Fit models produced in the company's plant in Brazil, Honda will switch production of about 30,000 to bioethanol cars.

The Brazilian government has mandated from 2008 that diesel-fuel vehicles such as trucks and buses have at least 2 percent vegetable oil added, in an effort to promote biofuel use. Currently, the market for flex vehicles is centered on Brazil, but with the Bush administration's call for diversified energy, flex may come into favor in bigger markets.

Japan, too, has taken steps to introduce, from April 2007, the earlier-mentioned ethanol petroleum, synthetic product, ETBE, with gasoline as a "biogasoline."

Running on Natural Gas

Most Japanese are familiar with the compressed natural gas (CNG) vehicle, since it got an early jump on fossil-fuel alternatives in Japan. Convenience-store chains across Japan, sensitive to the environmental concerns of their customers, converted to CNG-powered delivery trucks, sparking a CNG movement among major distribution companies.

The Japan branch of the World Wide Fund for Nature (WWF), one of the largest conservation nongovernment organizations in the world, issued a press release in February 2002 praising the parcel delivery company Sagawa Express for taking part in its CO_2 Reduction Program. The Tokyo-based Sagawa Express was teetering on the brink of oblivion in the early 1990s when it turned to "safety, environment, and service" as its operating slogan in 1998. The WWF release was effective in drawing attention to the company's activities.

"We raised consumer trust in our brand by taking part in the WWF program and efforts to reduce CO_2 in our operations. We looked to win over customers by introducing natural gas vehicles throughout our fleet and boosting our green image," notes Sagawa Express executive officer Kyoichi Bessho.

Sagawa CNG truck
Photograph courtesy of
Sagawa Express Co., Ltd.

After the signing of the Kyoto Protocol, Sagawa Express actively began introducing natural gas vehicles, with more than 26,000 by 2006, and reducing total CO_2 emissions in fiscal 2004 to 2.49 percent below 2002 levels. It achieved about half of that, approximately 4,295 tons, with the introduction of natural gas vehicles. The company aims to further reduce CO_2 emissions to 6 percent below 2002 levels by fiscal 2012. To achieve an approximate 50,000-ton reduction, Sagawa is replacing diesel trucks with some 4,500 more natural gas vehicles for a fleet of 7,000, and is also actively installing its own natural gas filling-stand infrastructure.

Natural gas is compressed and stored on board the vehicle, where an adjustment device is used to reduce pressure as the gas is fed into the engine. Noise and vibration are minimal, CO_2 emissions are even lower than those for hybrid and diesel-engine cars, and costs are reasonable. More vehicle fleet-dependent companies like Sagawa are adopting the technology.

Seeing this movement, some automakers are readying themselves to take special orders for new-model CNG vehicles. For example, Isuzu had been building 200–300 CNG vehicles a year since 1990, but switched focus to the production of the "Elf" (N-series), a light two-ton truck of the kind used by convenience-store companies, boosting production in 2004 to about 1,600 commercial vehicles. Toyota chimed in with their Dyna and Toyoace CNGs, and Nissan with its medium-duty CNG Condor truck.

U.S., China, India Commitments Unclear

By 2005, about 4.1 million natural gas vehicles were plying the world's roads, particularly in countries such as Argentina and Brazil. In Japan, there are still only about 300 natural gas filling stations, limiting the growth of natural gas vehicles to about 24,000 trucks and buses. Says a hopeful Tokyo Gas Co. vice president, Shigeru Kusano: "If the infrastructure is put in place, there is great potential for growth."

CNG auto rickshaw in New Delhi
Photograph courtesy of Bajaj Auto Ltd.

"New Delhi is one of the greenest cities in the world," declared the city's chief minister at the World Economic Forum held there in January 2006. "No city uses as much CNG as New Delhi." Even in New Delhi, where cows still block the way into Indira Gandhi International Airport, these past few years have seen an incredible rise in the number of passenger vehicles, but the main method of automotive transportation remains the three-wheeled "auto rickshaws," which run on CNG.

In the extended debate that followed ratification of the Kyoto Protocol, the question of gaining the cooperation of emerging countries such as China and India to take part in restricting greenhouse-gas emissions was left as a major upcoming theme, along with U.S. participation. At the World Economic Forum, New Delhi Summit, the arguments for and against India's participation grew heated. But while India's government leaders seem lukewarm about Kyoto Protocol participation, a concerted effort to use CNG show them to be independently serious about having cleaner air. Japanese upper-house councilwoman Junko Kawaguchi, who has held the posts of foreign minister and environment minister, says that "it is important for large countries like the U.S., China, and India, who are not signatories to Kyoto to aggressively implement global warming prevention programs of their own."

The Electric Car

The electricity-powered car, or carriage, is believed to have been first invented by Scotsman Robert Davidson in 1838, who used a battery-powered motor to power a vehicle up to a scintillating 4 miles per hour. Much simpler to build and operate than the steam or internal combustion engine, the EV didn't require any special technological innovation, and therefore competed head to head with steam- and gas-powered vehicles for supremacy as an automotive technology at the end of the nineteenth century. Another pioneer Ferdinand Porsche, the father of the VW Beetle, developed a two-passenger, front-wheel-drive EV with an in-wheel motor back in 1900.

EVs again garnered the spotlight in the late 1960s, when pollution from auto-tailpipe emissions was singled out as a major health problem. EVs began to be viewed as a reasonable choice for countering higher oil prices. More recently in the 1990s, when the California Air Resources Board issued its low-emissions mandate and automotive restrictions, EVs got a third look.

Honda's EV has already been discussed here at length, but the often overshadowed Japanese automaker, Mitsubishi, is also looking to use its own technological savvy to get ahead of the curve in EV technology. The company installed Takashi Nishioka from Mitsubishi Heavy Industries as chairman, and Osamu Masuko from Mitsubishi Corporation as president to form the core of a clean-energy strategy. It was clarified in the company's revival plan, which included rolling out new models.

"For Mitsubishi to survive, we need our own proprietary technologies. The EV holds out promise on a comprehensive basis from environment to safety and fuel efficiency. We definitely want to see production of an environmentally friendly car," stressed Masuko.

In-Wheel Motor a Proprietary Development

Mitsubishi attached in-wheel motors, powered by a lithium battery, to the rear wheels of its compact, Colt, in a prototype, and unveiled it as the Colt EV as part of the Mitsubishi Innovative EV strategy. It had a maximum output of 20 kilowatts and a maximum speed of 150 kilometers per hour (93.2 miles per hour). The company plans to increase in-wheel-motor output to a maximum 50 kilowatts, and to experiment with a high-performance, four-wheel-drive car. In 2005, Mitsubishi rolled out the compact crossover SUV Outlander, powered by a new high-performance, low-emissions, and low-fuel-consumption three-liter V6 MIVEC engine, and in 2006 the innovative mini-vehicle, the Mitsubishi "i", which won critical and commercial acclaim for its style and design. Mitsubishi is planning a battery electric version for release in 2010, along with plans to demo the "i" with a lithium battery. Both vehicles proved highly popular among Japanese consumers, proving that Mitsubishi retains the wherewithal to fight it out in the clean-car war.

Mitsubishi Colt EV
Photograph courtesy of Mitsubishi Motors Corporation.

Unlike conventional gasoline cars, EVs produce no direct emissions from their tailpipe. The only

Mitsubishi "i"
Photograph courtesy of Mitsubishi Motors Corporation.

threat they pose to the environment in terms of emissions would come from the generation of electricity needed to recharge the car, particularly if it comes from emission-emitting power plants. But wind and solar alternatives to electricity generation could decrease that ecological footprint even further. The absence of fuel costs has also prompted Fuji Heavy Industries, maker of Subaru automobiles, to get into the EV game as well. But Mitsubishi has established itself with in-wheel-motor technology. By directly attaching a motor to the wheel, and circumventing the transmission or drive shaft, power to the wheels can be very precisely controlled. And in-wheel motors also free considerable space for body layout and design.

Increasingly, the large energy capacity of lithium batteries means that they are being seen as the best choice for EVs, and Mitsubishi has been recruiting the help of its group affiliate, Mitsubishi Chemical Corp. A single charge of the

2003 Subaru R1e
Photograph courtesy of Fuji Heavy Industries, Ltd.

150-kilogram (330 pounds) lithium battery provides a driving distance of about 150 kilometers (93.2 miles), potentially twice the distance of a NiMH battery. Mitsubishi's current objective is to increase that distance, by 2010, to as much as 240 kilometers (149 miles). "The EV can get to the market quicker than the fuel-cell vehicle, which makes it realistic as a green car," says environment division chief, Eizo Tabo. "We're putting our effort into assuring reliability and cutting costs in our goal to make it a practical product."

The state of California, with its huge car market, once again used its zero-emission (electric) vehicle mandate in 1998 to bring auto companies back to the EV drawing board. But after it quickly became evident that a single charge of the battery could not provide the sufficient driving distance that people needed in their daily lives, coupled with EV technology still needing time to develop, many automakers began shifting their research budgets to hybrid and diesel alternatives. Eventually, California gave its blessing to hybrid cars on a exchange ratio with EVs at four hybrids for every EV. But Mitsubishi remains one auto company that doesn't plan to abandon its EV program for any reason.

Both Mitsubishi and Fuji Heavy Industries have set 2010 as the target year for groundbreaking EV rollouts. With the advent of the plug-in hybrid, the EV just might stick around for good this time.

Related Fronts I (Batteries)

Some of the biggest benefactors of the green-car war are component makers, particularly new entrants in the auto industry thanks to hybrid technologies. Those making batteries for powering motors are particularly busy. One of the forerunners is Panasonic EV Energy Co. (PEVE), jointly established in 1996 by Toyota and Matsushita Electric Industrial Co. Another leading competitor in the field is Sanyo Electric Co., which has amassed an impressive suite of technology in rechargeable batteries. They are joined by the likes of Hitachi Ltd. and NEC Corp., which are also hard at work developing lithium-ion batteries that can last longer and provide greater acceleration performance than NiMH batteries.

"Rechargeable batteries comprise one-third of the price of central components that go into the hybrid car. Our products are highly reliable, and we're constantly working to bring their costs down," said Mitsuru Homma, group executive of Sanyo's Power Solutions Group and president of its Mobile Energy Company. Homma is confident that the hybrid car has brought a renewed role for Sanyo, which commands a whopping near-50 percent global share of the rechargeable battery market, including nickel-cadmium and NiMH varieties, and is increasing that share for hybrid-car batteries.

Sanyo successfully developed the nickel-cadmium battery in 1964, using its own in-house technology. When it next succeeded in the development of the NiMH battery in 1990, it found a link to the auto industry. Up until the hybrid car, Sanyo's mainstay products had primarily been geared to digital cameras and power tools.

While Panasonic EV Energy provides Toyota with its hybrid batteries, Sanyo has been selling its products to Honda and Ford, climbing to second place behind PEVE, which at one point looked on the verge of monopolizing the market. Sanyo also has its sights set on providing batteries to Daimler and VW, and has signed an agreement with VW for joint hybrid NiMH battery development. The strength of Sanyo lies largely in proprietary bipolar plate-sintering technology, essentially making for long-lasting, high-endurance, high-output batteries. And Sanyo has made a name for itself by achieving high specification consistency and stability in mass production.

The future, at least in the near term, seems linked to lithium-ion battery technology as a key component in hybrid vehicles to come, so that is where Sanyo is investing its resources. In 2006, Sanyo built a pilot plant next to its Tokushima Factory for producing 1,000 lithium-ion units per month, and shipped samples to major automakers.

The global market for hybrid cars is estimated at a current value of 30 billion–40 billion yen (US$260 million–US$348 million). But it is expected to grow to 3 million vehicles and a valuation of about 400 billion yen (US$3.4 billion)—a tenfold increase by 2010. Sanyo wants to make sure it grabs the initiative in lithium batteries, which bid to figure largely in next-generation automotive technologies. Even so, the Osaka-based Sanyo Electric is struggling overall and is in the midst of a major corporate restructuring effort. Expectations of market growth in rechargeable batteries for hybrid vehicles should greatly benefit business prospects for Sanyo's Mobile Energy Company, however, which has its own hybrid-car rechargeable-battery division.

Giving chase in lithium-ion battery development are Hitachi and NEC. NEC has joined hands with Nissan to develop the technology jointly, and plans to produce and sell small- and large-capacity lithium-ion batteries by 2010. On a cubic-content basis, lithium-ion batteries carry larger electrical capacity than the NiMH batteries currently being installed in hybrid vehicles, and can be made to less than half the weight. If they can help make cars lighter, they'll boost fuel economy. But lithium-ion batteries have low ignition points, as has been seen with flaming laptops in 2006, leaving stability and cost as large issues for battery makers to overcome. Battery makers are, therefore, also looking for new solutions, such as the development of alternative materials to lithium.

Related Fronts II (Dies, Motors, Components)

The emergence of compact, lightweight yet highly efficient hybrid motors is also creating a high-profit industry. IC lead frame makers and other precision metals makers, that have built up their technological strength on thin-material processing, figure to play a prominent role in the automotive industry to come.

"Motor-core dies have been our specialty since our inception, and we can respond to any demand," boasts Mitsui High-tec, Inc. chairman, Yoshiaki Mitsui, 85, whose confidence is bolstered by his company having been in charge of motor-core production for the Prius since the outset. The company's technology for stamping highly conductive steel plating onto hair-thin micro motor core has been widely acclaimed. Currently, motor cores of up to 23 millimeters (0.9 inch) in outside diameter have been successfully made with 0.15-millimeter (0.0006 inch) thick material, and those of larger outside diameter are also available on demand.

A motor is built by stacking many thin magnetic plates. The thinner each plate is, the better the efficiency, so techniques are required to make the plates as thinly as possible. Half a millimeter (0.02 inch) was once seen as the limit, but Mitsui says he can now process plates as thin as 0.15 millimeter (0.006 inch). When core thickness is 5 centimeters (1.9 inches), 100 plates 0.5 millimeter thick can be stacked. But at 0.15 millimeters, that number swells to 333 plates. Not only does Mitsui need to hammer out more than 300 thin magnetic plates, but it has to do each one with great dispatch. The more silicon is used in the magnetic plates, the greater the performance. But a high level of technique is required, because they are exceedingly brittle.

Industrial Realignment on the Horizon

The first-generation Prius motor-core plates were 0.35 millimeter (0.014 inch) "thin." For the Harrier Hybrid (Lexus RX 400h) that debuted in 2005, there were 240 plates in the motor core, each 0.3 millimeter (0.012 inch) thin. To make the electric performance better in the future, these will have to be made even thinner, demanding a switch to a more amorphous material. Mitsui High-tec knows this, and is making preparations.

Visitors to the company's new metal-die plant in Kitakyushu can witness how a slight variance in temperature can greatly affect the elasticity of steel. There, it implements a temperature-control and humidity-control regime on a par with that of a semiconductor factory. Temperatures are maintained at 24°C (75.2F) plus or minus one degree, while humidity is maintained at 50 percent plus or minus 10 percent. The objective for free-floating dust and dirt is 0.5 microns or less per cubic foot, in line with U.S. federal standards, for what amounts to a thoroughly "clean room." The multiple thin magnetic plates that build cores were initially soldered together in the first Prius, but that changed with the Harrier Hybrid to a method of applying constant pressure. Wasteful processes are continuously removed to raise the level of precision.

"My role in life has been to oversee the evolution of metal-die precision. My constant challenge is to raise the precision of components, and build metal dies that stand the global test of quality," says the tireless octogenarian Mitsui.

Many other components have, of course, basked in the limelight of the hybrid and diesel car. Tamura Corp., specialist in ceramic condensers, is using its strengths in ceramic technology to enter the lithium-ion battery sphere. By the fall of 2008, Tamura plans to bring its power tools and electronic-assist bicycles to the market, and it hopes that that will lead to a future entry into hybrid-car components.

Investors are taking renewed interest in Japanese companies such as NGK Insulators, which globally manufactures ceramic catalyst carriers to convert HC, CO, and NO_x into harmless elements; and Ibiden Co., which makes diesel particulate filters. And there is a groundswell of industrial realignment taking place as the automotive component market expands in scope and breadth. Hitachi has made its automotive-machinery division, dealing in hybrid-car motors, a high-priority area, turning automotive-device maker Clarion into a consolidated subsidiary.

The investment fund RHJ International in 2003 purchased automotive component company Asahi Tec, which then acquired major U.S. automotive component maker and rival Metaldyne in 2006. Asahi Tec chairman Shoichiro Irimajiri, a former vice president at Honda, says, "Not only is global competition heating up in the automotive industry, but continued innovations in safety and environmental technologies will prove indispensable as well as lucrative. Finished automakers can't be expected to handle all the technological innovation they will require, all by themselves. That translates into an expanded role for component makers."

Tokyo Motor Show 2007

A futuristic array of electric, diesel, hybrid, flex, and fuel-cell vehicles was paraded at the 40th Tokyo Motor Show 2007, which opened on October 24 at the iconic, Fumihiko Maki-designed Makuhari Messe convention center just outside Tokyo in Chiba prefecture. The latest advances to the gasoline car were represented as well, but it was green technology overall that defined the show.

Perhaps the most conspicuous element was the absence of executives from the Big Three U.S. automakers, which helped to steer attention to how far Japanese carmakers were progressing on all environmental-technology fronts.

I came away impressed with the depth and breadth of technological strength that the Japanese auto industry has been stockpiling, owing in great part to a trend toward collaboration with blue-chip materials and electronics companies. Undoubtedly the most popular vehicles at the show were zero-emissions "personal city commuters," which, though kitschy, were designed in consideration of the heavy congestion of people and vehicles on Japanese roads. They truly brought into bold relief what I would label "meticulously targeted technologies," in which Japanese companies seem so strong.

Stealing a considerable share of the spotlight was the Toyota single-person EV, the i-REAL, trumpeted by president Katsuaki Watanabe as a "next-generation synthesis of man and machine." Basically, it is a moving bucket seat on three wheels, with the back wheel attached to the end of an extension that automatically retracts as speed decreases, changing the wheelbase of the vehicle so that at slow speeds, the driver/passenger is upright like a pedestrian, while at highway speeds, it hunkers down into a more elongated vehicular position with a lower center of gravity. It's a vehicle designed to be equally at home on sidewalks and bicycle lanes, as well as out on the open road, and comes equipped with a spate of safety features, such as periphery obstruction sensors, which detect and alert the driver to the presence of people and other objects through sound and vibration. Driver operation is conducted by way of the "by wire" technology employed in aviation, where driver movement is converted to electrical signals, rendering a steering wheel and connecting shaft to the wheels unnecessary.

Toyota i-REAL
Photograph courtesy of Toyota Motor Corp.

Toyota also used the event to announce its 1/X (one-xth) compact hybrid concept, so named because it purports to weigh as much as one-third of a Prius due to a body built of carbon fiber, requires only half as much fuel as a Prius to travel any given distance, and produces half the noise. It houses a gas engine plus a motor that can be recharged in the home as a plug-in hybrid. The technology promises a great boost to Toray Industries, Inc., which developed the carbon fiber that affords the vehicle both its strength and light weight. If the 1/X goes into production, Toray hopes to refine its expertise in casting and molding technologies.

Toyota has begun testing some of its plug-in hybrids on public roads, finding their motors capable of powering vehicles for 13 kilometers (8 miles) out of a three-to-four-hour battery charge. This eventually prompted Toyota to exhibit a concept plug-in hybrid at the show, the Hi-CT. Meanwhile, Toyota continues to push forward the hybrid technology that began with the Prius, extending it to more and more models, and looking to build upon its competitive edge in that market.

Toyota Hi-CT
Photograph courtesy of Toyota Motor Corp.

Battery development, however, remains critical for achieving success in both the hybrid and EV sphere, and Toyota's R&D collaboration with Matsushita in rechargeable batteries has proven a winning combination. Both companies have seen the need to deepen their relationship further, with mutual stakes, so that they can welcome other electronic component makers into the fold, particularly in the development of lithium-ion batteries, which offer the greatest electrical storage capacity to date. The strengthening of their relationship is serving as a cue to other automakers and electronics companies to consider crossover consolidation between industries.

Honda CR-Z
Photograph courtesy of Honda Motor Co.

Honda called attention to its green technologies with value-added pleasure, including hybrid sports car offerings in the FCX and CR-Z concepts, along with a more leisurely and comfort-oriented fuel-cell concept dubbed the "Puyo." The Puyo comes encased in a soft silicon resin that can be slightly depressed with a finger, and is designed to prevent injury to

Honda Puyo
Photograph courtesy of Honda Motor Co.

pedestrians in the event of a light scrape. "We want modes of mobility that work to soften the relationship between the automobile and both the environment and people," stressed Takeo Fukui, underscoring Honda's slightly different interpretation of automotive environment-friendliness compared with that of its competitors.

Nissan displayed the Pivo 2, an EV concept housing a large-capacity lithium-ion battery. Each tire is driven by a thin motor, enabling the wheels to turn 90-degrees to move the vehicle laterally. The Pivo 2 could radically alter the layout and dimensions of parking facilities, and render parallel parking a forgotten frustration. It also boasts an impressive driving distance of 120 kilometers (74.5 miles) on a mere twenty-minute battery recharge. Nissan partners with NEC in lithium-ion battery technology, which has succeeded in giving the new Pivo twice the electricity storage capacity of its first incarnation two years ago. Its thin yet powerful, in-wheel "3D Motor" was jointly developed by Nissan and Fujitsu. "For vehicles that produce absolutely no emissions, the EV turns

Nissan Pivo 2
Photography courtesy of Nissan Motor Co., Ltd.

out to be the best," notes Nissan president Carlos Ghosn. "It is set to drastically redefine mobility in the future, and Nissan plans to lead the EV age." Nissan is also slated to introduce to the Japanese market, in 2008, a clean diesel-engine vehicle jointly developed with Renault.

Keeping pace in the EV race, Mitsubishi unveiled an upgraded version of its electric iMiEV Sport concept, boasting improved driving and environmental perfor-mance. Adopting a con-trol system that individually imparts power and control to the four wheels to achieve sports-car-like driving perfor-mance, the iMiEV's most unique feature may lie outside the car, because its battery can be recharged "cordlessly" using special microwave technology developed by group company Mitsubishi Heavy Industries. Mitsubishi also plans to move up its planned release of an EV based on its light vehicle, the Mitsubishi "i", from 2010 to 2009, for a simultaneous rollout in both Japanese and over-seas markets. President Osamu Masuko said his company is eager to release the "i" ahead of schedule and show the world not only how envi-ronmentally friendly the car is, but how exceedingly fun it is to drive.

Subaru G4e
Photograph courtesy of Fuji Heavy Industries, Ltd.

Mazda RX-8
Photography courtesy of Mazda Motor Corporation.

Fuji Heavy Industries weighed in with a next-generation lithium-ion battery-powered EV called the Subaru G4e Concept, capable of running 200 kilometers (124 miles) on a single charge. The battery is stored under the floor, and Fuji Heavy Industries hopes it will dispel the notion that EVs are too heavy and defi-cient in cabin space.

Mazda, the Japanese affiliate of Ford, brought out its RX-8 Hydrogen RE, with patented hydrogen rotary engine. Mazda also announced it would be cooperating with the Norwegian government in promoting a hydrogen-energy infrastructure plan by providing hydrogen-powered cars.

Suzuki widened show visitors' eyes with its one-seater "personal mobility pod" concept called the PIXY, which can pair up with another pod, and dock inside another vehicle called the Suzuki Sharing Coach (SSC). It runs on a fuel cell, and travels at about the same speed as pedestrians, at 6 kilometers per hour, making it suited for use on sidewalks and even inside buildings. But it must undergo the transformer-like integration with the box-shaped SSC if it wants to reach highway speeds of 100 kilometers per hour (62 miles per hour). "We've proposed something that makes mobility a whole lot of fun," said Hiroshi Tsuda, Suzuki president.

Suzuki PIXY
Photograph courtesy of Suzuki Motor Corporation.

European automakers continued to promote their advances in diesel technology. Two days before the opening of the Tokyo Motor Show,

Mercedes F700
Photography courtesy of Daimler AG.

Daimler held a "Mercedes-Benz Symposium," and introduced its futuristic touring sedan, the Mercedes-Benz F700, housing an advanced internal combustion engine developed by Daimler called "Diesotto," which combines the lower emissions of a gasoline engine over diesel, with the lower fuel consumption of a diesel engine. As a 1.8-liter, four-cylinder engine, it emits 127 grams of CO_2 per kilometer (7.16 ounces per mile), gets 18.8 kilometers to the liter (44 miles per gallon), reaching a performance level on a par with the 3.5-liter, naturally aspirated V6 gasoline engines of the Mercedes S Series. Along with installing BlueTec in all of its Mercedes-Benz E Series vehicles, Daimler made clear its plan to integrate BlueTec with hybrid technology in its vehicles by 2010.

German counterpart BMW used the Tokyo Motor Show to display a hybrid SUV and redraw attention to its Hydrogen 7, a 7-Series sedan converted to run on liquid hydrogen. Swedish automaker Volvo, which it is rumored will be sold by Ford to BMW, exhibited its own home-rechargeable, plug-in hybrid.

Without a strong presence from the Big Three U.S. automakers, the Tokyo Motor Show 2007 really leaned toward Japanese ideas, giving the local players a chance to display the depth of their technological prowess and imagination. In 2007, the total value of shipments by the Japanese auto industry reached approximately 50 trillion yen, accounting for nearly 20 percent of Japanese industry overall. And this is a figure that is likely to rise as major electronic companies and materials makers begin to establish stronger relationships with automakers. The lead in the environmental technology that Japanese auto companies have managed to build can be traced to a great extent to the technological strength of other local industries, from electronics to chemicals. Considering the cost of research and the level of technology that will be required to survive in the auto industry, the coming convergence and synergies that will be reaped through these partnerships in the environmental technology sphere are sure to play a decisive role in determining which companies will emerge victorious in the years to come.

This is not to suggest that American auto companies are not serious about crafting their own winning strategies for greener cars. GM has begun road testing its much-anticipated EV, the Chevrolet Volt, and is due to go into production by the end of 2010. It is powered by a new lithium-ion battery purported to have a life of ten years. When the battery runs low on electricity, the engine is used as a recharge it. The engine is in use much less than with a hybrid, which has to combine the two power sources to meet different driving conditions. American automakers are aiming for mid-size-model price points for their home-rechargeable plug-in vehicles. The Volt can clearly outdistance Toyota-developed EVs, by running 40 miles on its battery alone, and is largely expected to be competitive with Japanese hybrids in the eco-car and fuel-efficiency realm.

Ford, meanwhile, has partnered with a major utility company in California to lay the groundwork for accelerating commercialization of its plug-in hybrid vehicles and building out the necessary infrastructure. Ford hopes to take EVs higher on the conservation scale by promoting better and more efficient use of the power grid, and employing its accumulated know-how in electrical technology to improve battery-recharging systems.

The Toyota Prius was considered a sleeper hit primarily because automakers hadn't quite realized how much American consumers were immediately willing to turn their concerns about the environment and rising oil prices into purchasing decisions. The market for hybrid vehicles in 2007 grew by 35 percent, or 340,000 units. By 2010, demand for hybrid cars is projected to account for approximately 5 percent of the total passenger-car market, or 800,000 vehicles. U.S. auto manufacturers, which for a time seemed to have abandoned the EV, are once again showing themselves eager to fast-track its development, and make a pre-emptive strike in the next round of the clean-car war.

Chapter 5

Winning Strategies

The Chinese Battlefront

The road to survival and leadership in the future global auto market is undoubtedly going through China. It is, after all, the world's second-largest market for automobiles after the U.S., and is closing in on number one fast. But anyone who has been to China recently would surely have been aghast at the traffic congestion.

Even on Beijing's main thoroughfare, Chang'an Avenue, at rush hour, one can expect to sit helplessly, choking on fumes and dust. The road infrastructure simply is not able to keep up with the rise in the number of automobiles.

"Beijing buses are slower than bicycles," said vice-minister of construction Qiu Baoxing at the National Conference of Public Transport Development in December, 2006. Buses in China's metropolitan areas average speeds of 10 kilometers per hour (6.2 miles per hour), considerably short of the 12 kilometers per hour (7.4 miles per hour) rate of bicycles. Average speeds on Beijing's principal roads have dropped in half in the past decade, with 60 percent of major intersections "seriously" clogged with traffic. Qiu, who waxes nostalgically about the capital's days as the "kingdom of bicycles," calls the congestion and accumulated exhaust an "urban and environmental disaster."

Toyota Tackles China's Environmental Problems

The Chinese authorities have at last begun pursuing pollution-control measures and looking into cleaner mobility methods, such as fuel-cell technology. From a management-strategy perspective, the key to preempting the welter of internal and foreign competitors rushing to the Chinese auto market successfully should lie in the country's ability to bring low-polluting and affordable compact cars to the masses. The major automakers of the world are already jostling for position as they increasingly stake their future growth on the colossally lucrative and largely untapped Chinese market, in what may shape into a war over "affordability and environmentalism."

"The Chinese and U.S. markets are very different," notes former Toyota China strategist Yoshimi Inaba. "Half of the Chinese auto market is made up of commercial vehicles, with the demand for compact and mini-cars being enormous. There is a growing interest, too, in green and energy-saving measures that combat rising air pollution and energy costs. Toyota has therefore decided to start selling the Prius in China, even if the market for it is still relatively immature. Toyota hopes, however, to begin carving out a name for itself as a pro-environment company in China.

Toyota launched its first overseas assembly of the Prius in China at the end of 2005, through a joint venture with China's FAW Corp. in Jilin province. Key components are imported from Japan, and assembled in China, with the retail price set at about that of the high-end Crown. As expected, sales have been slow due to the Prius' steep price tag. But Toyota views it as a strategy to gain an early foothold in the hybrid-car market to come in China, and will likely expand its hybrid lineup beyond the Prius.

Inaba, who earned an MBA degree from the Kellogg School of Management at Northwestern University near Chicago, is a pro-American thinker, who has served as president and CEO of Toyota Motor Sales, U.S.A., and head of Toyota's U.S. headquarters in Torrance, California. Using the strong network of relationships he has forged in U.S. government and financial circles, Inaba has been an instrumental figure behind Toyota's surge in North America, with the success of the Prius being among his finest achievements. Launching a preemptive strike with the hybrid car in China was his next mission.

"In the U.S., the Prius found support among a public willing to buy greener automobiles even if it meant a premium price tag," says Inaba. "The environmental movement in China has yet to reach that level, but is steadily growing in metropolitan areas such as Beijing, Shanghai, and Guangzhou."

Etsuo Hattori was raised in China and knows the country well. As chief representative of Toyota's China office, he was an early advocate of environmental pollution controls in China. "[Although] air pollution in China came mainly from the smoke of factories and houses... in recent years... automobile emissions have been seriously increasing," said Hattori in a speech at the Boao Forum for Asia's annual conference held in April 2005. "The Chinese government should restrain the production of high-fuel-consumption vehicles and critical vehicle-exhaust emissions by formulating restrictive regulations and high-tax policies, and should work to popularize eco-friendly cars by formulating an incentive tax policy aimed at addressing energy savings and decreased emissions across China."

Invited back as a speaker to the same conference the following April, Hattori cited Chinese production of the Prius as an example of the kind of efforts China should encourage. A Chinese businessman later asked him if he thought local companies had the technological savvy to begin producing hybrid cars. Hattori seemed to think so.

Only three months earlier at the Detroit Auto Show, Zhejiang Geely became the first Chinese auto company to display a car at a major North American auto venue. Chinese companies have been increasing their market share in the home market, and are already aggressively looking to sell their products abroad, including the Great Wall Motor Co. and Chery Automobile Co., which accounts for 7 percent of the Chinese passenger-car market. In environmental technologies, Chinese automakers still have considerable ground to make up on their Western counterparts, but this is a deficit that might quickly be erased by sheer business growth and, perhaps, a few shrewd partnerships. At the time the English version of this book was being compiled, speculation was rife that Chrysler would be sold to a Chinese automaker.

In October 2006, I had an opportunity to visit China on a mission of managers, academics, and journalists led by Japan–China Economic Association director Kenjiro Ogata, in which we toured the factories of various automakers that had begun operations in China.

Toyota has been producing Camry sedans at Guangzhou Toyota Motor Co. (GTMC) since May 2006. The factory sits adjacent to the expanding port of Guanghzou, and across the highway from an industrial park that houses a supplier consortium, including the Toyota group's Denso and Aisin Seiki. Toyota has dug two tunnels under the highway to facilitate the just-in-time supply system, in which customized transport trollies haul in requisite volumes of components every two minutes. It is a Toyota production system designed to maximize efficiency and reduce cost. Workers pull the components they need straight from the trollies onto the assembly line. By dispensing with forklifts and shortening conveyance distances, the risk of accidents such as dropped parts has been greatly reduced.

"If an idea arises that could streamline the process further, we try it," said GTMC president Toru Kuzuhara. The sight of women workers deftly carrying out the work at GTMC prompted Toyota chairman and current advisor Hiroshi Okuda, to comment that Japan, too, should rethink the role of women in the workplace. Toyota processes, planted in China, are helping to produce new value for the company.

Honda's Green Factories

Honda was actually the first among Japanese automakers to establish a joint venture with a Chinese company back in 1998. Splitting the investment 50–50 with the Guangzhou Automobile Group, Honda began building the Accord, the Odyssey, and the Fit in China. By 2005, Guangzhou Honda was churning out 240,000 cars a year, making it one of the five leading producers and marketers of automobiles in China—a list that includes industry leader Shanghai General Motors Co., and Shanghai Volkswagen Co.

Guangzhou Honda also boasts an eco strategy that meets the "Euro4" emissions standards, which are, at least for the moment, tougher than those of China. But the Chinese government is steadily strengthening its environmental regulations.

"The competition among auto companies here is intensifying, and will be increasingly fought over green technologies," explained Guangzhou Honda president Sho Minekawa. "China's emissions standards in the urban areas are still at Euro 2 and 3 levels in outlying areas, but she is already the world's second-largest auto market. So we went the extra mile to clear the tough Euro4 standards for our engines in lieu of the inevitable landscape, and as part of our overall efforts to thoroughly implement our environment and energy conservation strategy."

In September 2006, Guangzhou Honda completed its second assembly plant, and began producing the Accord, boosting the company's annual production capacity to 360,000 units. At the tape-cutting ceremony in front of a gaggle of local government officials and Guangzhou Automobile Group executives, Honda president Takeo Fukui proudly feted the new "Green Factory" as built to maximize environmental conservation and operational efficiency. It employs a full water-reuse and recirculation system with absolutely no external drainage of factory water.

Minekawa used the event to reassert the penetration of the Honda way as a key to the success of Guangzhou Honda. "The first step in working together is for everyone to understand and come to cherish what Honda stands for.

Nissan, too, is high on China. Although sales numbers in 2006 continued on a downward trend, dipping below previous-year levels both at home and in principal markets abroad, including North America and Europe, sales have been growing briskly in China. In 2003, Nissan formed a joint venture with the Dongfeng Motor Corp., one of China's "Big Five" automakers, to create the Dongfeng Motor Co. Ltd., which began production on the Nissan Tiida compact car. Through its platform-sharing agreement with Renault, Nissan also used China to launch what it has dubbed a "new global strategic car," a seven-seat minivan named Livina Geniss, currently being manufactured by Dongfeng Motor Co. China.

Chinese authorities are looking to rival Detroit by building a massive auto manufacturing city in the Huadu district of Guangzhou. It is already home to the "Big Three" Japanese auto companies and parts suppliers. Japanese component makers Calsonic Kansei Corp. and Unipres Corp. have opened up shop, primarily to serve Nissan. They hope to drive costs down by doing everything locally, from as early as product planning and design. The Huadu auto city is also expecting the arrival of Renault in the near future, and has enthusiastically set aside a vast tract of land for the French auto maker and related automotive concerns.

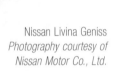

Nissan Livina Geniss
*Photography courtesy of
Nissan Motor Co., Ltd.*

Local Chinese auto companies, meanwhile, are bracing themselves for the competition to heat up. At the Beijing International Automotive Exhibition, held in November 2006, China's largest homegrown auto manufacturer, Chery, not only showed off a complete line of ten new and original models, but also a hybrid and diesel car.

Chery was founded in 1998, and scored a huge hit in 2003 with its QQ, a compact passenger "city car" selling for about 40,000 renminbi (about US$5,300) in China. But in the early days, China's homegrown auto development effort came with its share of controversy and skepticism as well. GM filed a lawsuit against Chery for allegedly copying a mini-car it had developed with its South Korean affiliate, Daewoo Motors.

China is gradually, however, acquiring the automotive savvy to produce unquestionably original products, often recruiting foreign talent such as Italian auto designers. If they strengthen their position in environmental technologies, they will certainly become a major force to be reckoned with among the automotive players of the world, and relatively soon.

Chinese Government and Scholars Turn Green

On that same mission in October 2006, I had the privilege of taking part in the Japan-China Entrepreneurs Forum on Environmental issues—Corporate Growth and Environmental Protection, where I was surprised to learn about the rapidly growing advocacy and penetration of environmental protection inside China.

Dr. Miao Chang is director and senior research fellow of the Division of Environmental Management and Policy at Tsinghua University, in Beijing. "No one has made much of the environment until now, not companies, citizens, not even the media. As a result, social monitoring of the environment has been extremely weak. But ever since a chemical explosion at a petrochemical plant led to the contamination of the Songhua river in 2005, there have been environmental accidents occurring at a rate of about once every two days. China's rapid rate of growth has clearly sent the country into a public pollution stage like that which Japan experienced during its rapid expansion in the 1960s and 1970s."

A Tsinghua University Center for Business Research official pointed out that "businesses aren't looking to maximize short-term profits, but instead to raise intrinsic value. Contributing to society through a value network leads to a company's growth and sustainability. We need to have a shared perception of how we can conserve and protect the environment as a natural resource."

Among the 1,200 principal rivers across China, about 70 percent, or upward of 850 of them, are reported to be polluted. Of the 47 major cities, 22 of them are said to have contaminated drinking water, leaving 23 million people with an insufficient supply of drinkable water. On top of that, 30 percent of the nation's land area is undergoing rapid desertification.

I remember finding myself staring blankly down at a dry riverbed from the infamous Marco Polo Bridge, site of the first clash of the Second Sino-Japanese War in 1937. The river across which Chinese and Japanese troops had squared off now exposed a couple of abandoned and splintered boats.

The Chinese undoubtedly know more than anyone how serious the situation has become.

The automobile market in China reached approximately 7 million vehicles in 2006, passing previous number two, Japan, and lining up squarely behind the U.S. as the second-largest auto market in the world. With such a rapid pace of motorization, it is no wonder Chinese authorities are making environmental policy a higher priority. With increased demand spawning newer and greater production capacity by more and more auto-market players, Chinese authorities have begun to fear a situation of massive oversupply. From the end of 2006, China began restricting new plant construction, in addition to enacting other structural reforms in the automotive industry. The principal aim was to elicit realignment among the crush of more than 100 auto companies vying for market position, and to see those that can't meet environmental demands weeded out.

The Eleventh Five-Year Plan, launched in 2006, includes an emphasis on promoting energy conservation and introducing renewable energy, and a policy shift away from putting the economy ahead of all else, to one of resource savings and environmental consciousness. Although it put no enforcement measures in place, the government plans to introduce multifaceted measures such as tax incentives for low-environmental-load businesses, along with promoting environmental impact assessments and encouraging greater public scrutiny of environmental impact.

In November 2006, China's State Environmental Protection Agency published its "green procurement inventory" for government procurement that stipulated government cars be chosen from among nine specific brands, including Peugeot and Nissan vehicles, the Honda CR-V, and the Audi A6 and A4 series. Conspicuously left off the list was the VW Santana, assembled by Shanghai Automotive Industry Corp. Alhough previously the government vehicle of choice, the Santana's exclusion served as a warning to companies that fail to be aggressive about reaching the new environmental bar.

Furthermore, China's National Development and Reform Commission established targets for domestic sales of gasoline at a greater than 50 percent ethanol-gasoline mix by 2010. In the Eleventh Five-Year Plan for Ethanol and Automotive Ethanol Fuel, the ethanol-fuel industry's five-year roadmap includes tax cuts for ethanol producers, with the hope of stimulating the spread and expansion of domestic biofuel production.

The Toyota "Meme"

Outside China, there are other longer-term factors that look to augur the success of auto companies such as Toyota and Honda in the coming new automotive paradigm. Whatever the industry, companies must increasingly be able to grasp the important changes taking place in the world, and be willing to adjust accordingly and quickly if they hope to survive intense competition and sustain their growth.

In February 2005, when queried about the reasons for handing over the Toyota reins to executive vice president Katsuaki Watanabe, Hiroshi Okuda said, "Toyota has grown very big, and though we may not be suffering from the large corporation disease yet, I can feel its oncoming symptoms. We need to get younger in the organization if we are to move forward."

At the time of this announcement, Okuda was 72 years old, outgoing president Fujio Cho was 68, and Watanabe was 62. Only ten years ago, almost to this date, Hiroshi Okuda had been 62 and found himself suddenly catapulted to president. After Okuda relinquished the top post to Fujio Cho in 1999, he assumed chairmanship of the *Nihon Keidanren*, or Japan Business Federation, where he

Katsuaki Watanabe
Photograph courtesy of Toyota Motor Corp.

seemed the perfect figurehead to represent all Japanese industry. After Okuda's departure from the helm of Toyota, Cho went on as president to craft important alliances in Europe and China, and expand consolidated sales under a successful global strategy. But it has become an ironclad rule at Toyota that a president steps aside when the time comes, and gives way to those below. Although Cho was considered a very capable leader, he too was no exception. Only honorary chairman Shoichiro Toyoda has retained some measure of continued stewardship over what has been his family estate for more than half a century. The rule is not codified, but anyone who rises from the ranks of the organization to the presidency will, when the time seems right, hand over the reigns of power sooner, rather than later. So when Cho had completed six years of executive leadership, he stepped down.

Watanabe, who succeeded Cho, was born on February 13, 1942. A graduate of Okazaki High School in Aichi prefecture, he matriculated to the esteemed Keio University, and graduated with a degree in economics. In 1964, he entered what was then still the Toyota Motor Company, working in procurement, administration and rising to economic planning division chief, before being named to the board in 1992. In 2001, Watanabe became one of seven executive vice presidents at Toyota. Having accumulated plenty of leadership experience working alongside several Toyota presidents, he had no qualms about declaring himself a "preacher of crisis vigilance." It was, indeed, a quality that was best suited for presiding over one of the world's largest auto companies: a strong sense of urgency and mission to keep the company moving, but also a great respect for continuity.

There are very few companies that handle the leadership succession process as smoothly as Toyota. Japanese like to call it the "passing of the baton." It involves strong communication, concerted education and training, and a firmly shared set of corporate beliefs that course through the veins of each successive president. Looking back over its history, Toyota has always been blessed by solid, unwavering leadership.

The Toyota *Koryo*

As Toyota grows and expands around the world, it is the *koryo* (literally, "main points"), which serves as the company creed to be imparted to all employees. Kiichiro and Risaburo Toyoda co-developed the *koryo* by compiling the core principles and beliefs of their father, Sakichi, and announced them on the sixth anniversary of his death. They are:

- Contribute to the development and welfare of the country by working together regardless of position, in faithfully fulfilling your duties.
- Remain at the vanguard of the times through endless creativity, inquisitiveness, and pursuit of improvement.
- Be practical and avoid frivolity.
- Be kind and generous; strive to create a warm, homelike atmosphere
- Be reverent, and show gratitude for things great and small in thought and deed.

These five principles, taken together as a whole, have been passed down through the Toyota group as moral guideposts governing the corporate life of all its employees.

In 2001, these principles were re-expressed as the Toyota Way. This was done because the company's philosophy needed to be more effectively communicated to employees and partners all around the world. Within the two main pillars of "Continuous Improvement" and "Respect for People," Toyota's basic principles are defined as "challenge", "*kaizen*" (improvement), "*genchi genbutsu*"—essentially going and seeing for oneself what is happening at the shop floor or in the local market, "respect," and "teamwork."

With a global workforce numbering about 300,000, the influence Toyota's "founding fathers" have over the company as its cohesive glue is immeasurable. In addition to the Toyoda family's active involvement throughout the company's history, all the lessons and teachings that were learned during the most critical and defining moments of Toyota's past are intentionally handed on to succeeding generations through a management-placement system overtly designed to put those most qualified to serve as veritable "crisis awareness missionaries" in strategic points throughout the organization.

Toyota employees have often been accused of being "*kintaro*" candy, a hard cylindrical sweet that reveals the same face inside, wherever one may bisect it. But because Toyota has been able to establish a firm method for passing down the experience of its past companywide, the giant auto company has been able to demonstrate surprising spiritual fortitude, whether on the offensive or defensive.

When Watanabe was named Toyota's president, I was in Stuttgart, Germany, listening to DaimlerChrysler announce its yearly results. When it came time for questions and answers, I asked Jurgen Schrempp what he thought of the new personnel change at Toyota, to which he remarked, "Toyota never fails to field a wonderful team."

The generational changing of the guard occurs, quite ceremoniously, at the presidential level and at the executive vice presidential level, with eight senior managers moving up the ladder. In recent years, the average age of the executive vice presidents has been actively lowered from 63.8 years to 57.9 to invigorate management.

On a weekly business documentary program I co-host on television, which examines the corporate DNA of companies that have successfully endured the devastation of the bubble and the severity of global competition, I had the privilege of asking Toyota chairman Cho what he believed was the secret to Toyota's strength. "Properly transmitting the venture spirit that founded Toyota," was his reply.

The program is called *Meme's Adventure*, where "meme" is defined as an idea that is passed from one human generation to another. It is the cultural equivalent of a gene. The "meme" of Kiichiro Toyoda has been dutifully relayed to successive generations with great care and deliberate attention. For the leadership of arguably the world's best company to continue to subscribe to this "venture spirit", across borders and generations, attests to the survival strength of the Toyota DNA, as embodied in the vision of Kiichiro Toyoda. He, therefore, warrants further description.

Free to pursue automobiles

Kiichiro Toyoda was born on June 11, 1894, in Shizuoka prefecture, west of Tokyo, in a coastal city situated on a narrow strip of land between the Lake Hamanako, and the Pacific Ocean now called Kosai Yamaguchi. It is also the birthplace of his father, Toyoda Automatic Loom Works, Ltd. founder Sakichi Toyoda. Kiichiro was Sakichi's first-born son. The family lived in a humble, four-room farmhouse, with traditional straw-thatched roof and dirt floors. He lived together with his uncles Sasuke and Heikichi, Sakichi's two younger brothers. Heikichi would later become Toyota Motors' auditor and father to future company president Eiji Toyoda. The home and buildings around it were restored in 1974, and turned into the Toyota Kuragaike Commemorative Hall, in commemoration of Toyota's 10 millionth vehicle.

The Toyoda family had for generations been peasant farmers who supplemented their income through carpentry. After the Meiji Revolution and the opening up of Japan to the outside world many former retainers of the toppled Tokugawa government followed their *shogun* from Edo (Tokyo) back to their original domains in Shizuoka. They settled in reclaimed homesteads close to where the Toyoda family lived, in stately abodes dubbed "warrior-class mansions," and sent many of their number into local politics and

Kiichiro Toyoda
Photograph courtesy of Toyota Motor Corp.

education. When a shipyard for the construction of steamships was built in a nearby village, it piqued the interest of a very naturally enterprising young man, Sakichi Toyoda, who often visited the docks to watch the ships being built, and who quickly began nurturing an interest in propulsion or motive power.

Sakichi had grown up watching his mother on the weaving loom, and wondered why nobody tried to make improvements to what seemed a very inefficient process. The electric motor gave him the inspiration to search for that answer himself. In 1890, Sakichi traveled to Tokyo for the third national industrial exhibition to observe machine-made goods, and came away with his eyes opened to the wondrous fruits of the industrial enlightenment, such as large steam engines and steel machine equipment. This hardened his resolve to become an "inventor." Sakichi poured his energies into the study and development of a new concept for the weaving loom, completing it and earning his first patent for a wooden loom in 1891.

With conventional hand looms, one hand threads the weft through the warp yarn through the use of a shuttle, while the other hand essentially readies the thread, and does the weaving. But Sakichi's loom sought to handle those two processes simultaneously with one hand, along with reducing irregularities in the weave for gains in both efficiency and quality. But because the process was still to be done by human hand, dramatic improvements in efficiency could not be expected. It wasn't until two years after the birth of his first son Kiichiro, in 1896, that Sakichi would complete a working prototype of a power loom.

Sakichi spent so much time away from home during the conception and design of his power loom that his first wife, Tami, eventually left him. Kiichiro was therefore raised by his paternal grandparents. Sakichi would later marry a woman named Asako from the same village, and move to Nagoya. The daughter he had with her, Aiko, would grow up and marry future Toyota Motor Company's first president, Risaburo Toyoda.

Kiichiro grew up an outwardly reticent and introverted boy in contrast to his father. Throughout grade school, Kiichiro played mostly with his stepsister Aiko, five years his younger, and could be found reading to her almost every night. His father Sakichi had by then established his reputation as a successful inventor and entrepreneur, and in 1907, when Kiichiro was entering secondary school, the Toyoda Loom Works company was established with help from the Mitsui & Co., Ltd. which, thanks to Sakichi's inventions, was banking on a growth in its domestic cotton production and exports to China. Sakichi was installed as the company's executive managing director, but soon found himself at odds with fellow managers. Sakichi placed a premium on tireless research, making improvements and reflecting those in frequent new products that could replace old technology. The company president and others, on the other hand, were more interested in mass-producing low-cost goods. Due in part to Sakichi's habit of spending the company's money on various inventions that would never come into practical use, the company's performance eventually declined, and Sakichi was forced to resign. He used the free time to travel to Europe and the U.S. for an inspection tour, returning fortified in his belief that his automatic loom was superior to any in the West, while at the same time astounded by the incredible motorization of American society owing to the automobile.

Desiring to run his own company, and seeing the need to produce his own quality thread, Sakichi, in 1911, built a fully fledged spinning factory on the west side of Nagoya called Toyoda Automatic Weaving, which would be reorganized as Toyoda Boshoku Corp., a textile-spinning and weaving company now serving as a global automotive-components company under the Toyota group.

In 1914, Kiichiro graduated from junior high school and gained entry into the elite Kyusei Higher School Number 2, which offered specialized education in engineering. There he made lasting friends, and found an environment that was conducive to study. Kiichiro took especially to learning about machine drafting and design. In 1917, he gained admission to the country's most prestigious Tokyo Imperial University (University of Tokyo), where he majored in mechanical engineering, and reveled in mechanics classes having to do with motor conduction and associated mechanical frameworks. He became profoundly interested in engines, not only in how they were built, but also in the mechanics of power generation. During school breaks, Kiichiro would find himself touring his father's factories with rapt attention.

In 1921, Kiichiro returned to Nagoya, where he joined Toyota Boshoku, and was put in complete charge of manufacturing and technology. Already serving as Sakichi's deputy at the company was Kiichiro's brother-in-law, Risaburo, who after marrying Aiko had entered his name in the Toyoda family register, and was managing the day-to-day affairs of the company from sales to accounting. Risaburo, although not related to Sakichi by blood, was for all intents and purposes treated with rights of primogeniture because he was older than Kiichiro. Business had boomed during World War I for Sakichi's company, which had advanced into the lucrative cotton-spinning business. Kiichiro just happened to be in Tokyo when the Great Kanto Earthquake of 1923 struck, devastating much of the greater Tokyo metropolitan region and leaving nearly 150,000 people dead in its wake. But he came away from that disaster thoroughly impressed with the role that the automobile played afterward as a makeshift replacement for public transportation. Twice, Kiichiro would travel to the U.S. and Europe, where he could see the great advances of the automobile age unfolding right before his eyes.

Kiichiro's first overseas tour came in 1921 at the age of 27. He was joined by Risaburo and Aiko on a journey that took them first to the U.S., and then to the U.K., where they would learn about shop-floor manufacturing through a factory training program at what was the world's biggest textile-machinery maker, Platt Brothers of England. Upon his return to Japan in 1922, Kiichiro took a wife in 27-year-old Hatako, daughter of Shinshichi Iida, founder of the Takashimaya clothing store in Kyoto, and now the major department-store chain, Takashimaya Co. When Sakichi exhorted Kiichiro to "devote all his energies to the textile business," Kiichiro obeyed, devoting himself particularly to development of the automatic loom. In 1924 came the completion of what Sakichi referred to as the "completely automatic loom" in the Type G automatic loom with nonstop shuttle-change motion, capable of operating at high speed without stoppage. The patent was listed as belonging to Kiichiro Toyoda. Japanese-made cotton fabric had found strong buyers in China, and Sakichi wasted no time in building a textile plant in Shanghai, moving there for what he planned would be an extended period. Once work on the above-mentioned Type G loom was nearly finished, Kiichiro left to join his father in Shanghai as an equipment technician. He didn't stay long, however, returning to Japan the next year in 1924 to begin construction on a large-scale automatic-loom assembly plant in a small town 20 miles from Nagoya called Kariya, which two years later would become the Toyoda Automatic Loom Works, Ltd. (now Toyota Industries Corp.). In late 1924, Kiichiro would also celebrate the birth of his second child and first son, future Toyota president Shoichiro. This was also the year that American auto manufacturer Ford began assembling automobiles in Yokohama.

Mass production of the Type G loom brought Toyoda Automatic Loom Works international attention. And this time it was the former industry mentor, Platt Brothers, that came calling with an interest in purchasing the Toyoda patent. In 1929, Kiichiro set off on his second tour of the U.S. and the U.K., this time with the expressed purpose of concluding a patent-transfer agreement with Platt Brothers, negotiations that were taking place against the backdrop of a worldwide depression. Kiichiro had first gone to the U.S. to find buyers for his patent, but couldn't get an acceptable price. By the time he got to the U.K., he agreed to give Platt Brothers exclusive manufacture and sales rights for £100,000. The payment of royalties became a bone of contention for some time afterward, and was ultimately settled at a reduced rate in 1934. But Kiichiro is said to have found the amount sufficient to use as start-up capital for a new venture he had been nurturing. The rapid decline of the textile industry in both the U.S. and the U.K. and the growing ranks of the unemployed around this time led Kiichiro to fear for the future of textile machinery, and he felt he would need to go in a new direction upon his return home. For Kiichiro, the direction was clear. In April 1930, he began research into automobile production, and succeeded in building a small prototype engine that could be attached to a vehicle by the Australian Smith Motor Co. Kiichiro believed that by developing a small, low-cost engine, he could prove to others in the company that building automobiles was within their realm of possibility.

In October 1930, Sakichi Toyoda, recipient of the Imperial Order of Merit for his contributions to Japanese industry, died at the age of 63. By this time, orders for Type G looms had rapidly decreased amid an industrywide recession. And with labor unrest developing in the face of factories closing, Kiichiro and Risaburo decided to use some of the royalties they'd received from Platt Brothers to distribute to employees a special bonus designed to restore morale and unity. And then, after earning consent from Risaburo to go ahead with his automobile-manufacturing concept inside Toyoda Automatic Loom Works, Kiichiro added to the company's business profile "the manufacture and sales of motors and motor-driven carriages or transport machines."

Kiichiro wasn't alone in his vision, however. Demand for automobiles was soaring, and scores of companies and industrialists had already turned their attentions to production of a domestically made vehicle. But now free to devote his energies to building automobiles, Kiichiro began producing a variety of different engine prototypes, while ordering various automobile parts and meticulously researching automotive-design methods and materials. One question that became a particular obsession and challenge for him was how to secure high quality cast iron, which would constitute the greatest material concern. Kiichiro sealed himself off in a corner of a factory behind plywood walls, so that he and his team could work in secrecy. But in 1932, Kiichiro found himself beaten to the punch. The first Japanese-built prototype passenger car was unveiled not far away. It was a seven-seater called the Atsuta, and was built at the behest of the Nagoya city mayor who, in hoping to make his city the "Detroit of Japan," had called upon a consortium of five locally based companies to build Japan's first homespun automobile. It was based on the popular Nash passenger cars built by Nash Motors, forerunner to the American Motors Corporation. His feet now to the fire, Kiichiro ramped up efforts to enter the now newborn domestic auto market. In September 1933, Kiichiro established an automobile division inside Toyoda Automatatic Loom Works.

Kiichiro had long set his sites on building a "people's car," much like those of American automakers Ford and Chevrolet. The Tobata Casting Co., Ltd., a cast-iron and auto-parts manufacturer, had purchased from "Datson" (later changed to "Datsun") the rights to manufacture a small passenger car, while other Nagoya-based companies were planning to build large trucks and buses. Outside Toyoda Automatic Loom Works, there seemed to be little movement in terms of producing a passenger car for the masses à la Ford or Chevrolet. From autumn through to the winter of 1933, Kiichiro brought into the Kariya plant a 1933 model Chevrolet, and pored over every last detail. He began patterning his engine on a Chevrolet and his body on a DeSoto. In December, news arrived that Tobata had conducted its groundbreaking ceremony on the factory site where it would begin manufacturing and selling its Datsons, and that it would rename itself the Jidosha Seizo Company (automobile manufacturing), joining forces with the Nihon Sangyo Co. (Japan Industries). On December 30, 1933, Toyoda added automobiles as an official company business.

The previous month, Kiichiro had asked local government officials to find him a potential new factory site, and by December 1935 had a 472-acre plot of land at his disposal, massive by any standards. Kiichiro also sent one of his experts to the U.S. to study automobile-manufacturing processes, as well as to procure necessary machinery for automobile-prototype production. He went headhunting, successfully recruiting people such as Shotaro Kamiya, who had experience in GM vehicle sales, and engineers who had taken part in building the Atsuta car. In September 1934, a metal-casting core arrived from the U.S., essential for use in the manufacture of cylinder blocks, and allowing him to successfully build a water-cooled, straight six-cylinder engine faithfully copied from a Chevrolet, and dubbed the Type A. It would be Toyota's first engine.

Kiichiro could not, however, produce an engine that satisfied him in terms of horsepower, dampening his aims of soon rolling out five vehicles a day. In June, the Jidosha Seizo Co. had changed its name to Nissan Motor Co., and in April 1935 at its Yokohama factory, the first Datsun sedan rolled off the assembly line. Feeling the pressure of competition, Kiichiro drew from British and American technical journals, and changed the cylinder's head shape, resulting fortuitously in increased engine horsepower. He

1934 Chrysler Airflow
Photography courtesy of Randy Stern.
This image is licensed under Creative
Commons Attribution 2.0 License.

was satisfied. And in May 1933, Toyota completed its first prototype passenger car, the A1, modeled extensively on the Chrysler Airflow, followed by the model G1 truck prototype in August.

The Japanese government passed the Automobile Manufacturing Industries Act that same month, giving promising companies the green light to start mass-producing automobiles to meet growing public demand, and to prevent American monopolization of the auto market. Toyota was one of the approved companies, and now it was time for the company to begin building up a track record. But Toyota had not yet established a sales system. There was dissatisfaction within the company toward earmarking more money to the automobile division, even though in the end Kiichiro and Risaburo decided to invest additional resources to the venture. Although they had yet to move to full-scale production, Kiichiro convened a meeting of sales managers to hammer out an organizational plan for future sales. This was followed by the announcement of a type AA passenger vehicle as an improvement over the A1, and an aggressive effort to draw attention to the vehicle. In 1936, Toyota and Nissan were the first two domestic companies to be sanctioned under the newly enacted Automobile Manufacturing Industries Act. Perhaps due to the heavy risk involved, all the Nagoya-based companies that had previously been working on automobile initiatives fell into oblivion. Kiichiro, on the other hand, to demarcate his move into mass production of automobiles further, decided to spin off the automobile division from Toyota Automatic Loom Works, and set up an independent company called "Toyota Motor Co., Ltd."

Toyota AA
Photograph courtesy of
Toyota Motor Corp.

The new company's inaugural general meeting took place on August 27, 1937 at the headquarters of Toyota Boshoku in Nagoya. Risaburo Toyoda was its acting president, with Kiichiro taking the position of vice president, even though it would be the 43-year-old Kiichiro who would effectively be in charge. Toyota Boshoku took a 50 percent stake in the company, investing a large portion of the wealth it had amassed through the manufacture and sales of its Type G looms. Kiichiro clarified the new company's organizational structure to consist of technical, operational, and design divisions, in addition to a research arm, which in addition to developing the automobile was tasked with a wide range of objectives, including research into metals and thermodynamics. A groundbreaking ceremony for the new Koromo Plant came on

September 29, 1937, one month after Toyota Motor was born. Construction on the facility that would eventually become Toyota Motor headquarters began, involving the use of the latest machine tools brought in from the West, while construction cranes, large and small, erected a pressing plant and foundry. A system was devised to ensure that not a single nut or bolt went to waste, instead Toyota would procure them on an "as needed" basis, marking the birth of the famous Toyota "just-in-time" production method. The Koromo Plant was completed on November 3, 1938, and it is the day Toyota marks as its founding. Kiichiro pulled the switch and the factory went into operation.

Automobile production didn't exactly follow the course that Kiichiro had hoped for. Initial plans called for an output of 200 vehicles per month, but the militarized Japanese government, now rapidly placing the country on a war footing, wanted ten times that production capability, at 2,000 vehicles per month. This put enormous pressure on Toyota's ability to control for defects and ensure parts procurement. The government was also more interested in the production of trucks and buses over passenger cars, forcing Kiichiro to put his dream of building a "people's car" on hold. In 1941, he assumed the company's presidency, and became its chief executive both in name and substance. But with the rapid militarization of the economy, Kiichiro saw his grip on the business increasingly being usurped by the government. In 1943, the Munitions Corporation Law wrested management and substantive control of the company away from Kiichiro.

No sooner had the war ended, with defeat for Japan in August 1945, than Kiichiro immediately moved to set up a voluntary-based automobile manufacturers' association with the approval of GHQ (the U.S.-led occupation authority headed by General Douglas MacArthur). Toyota also made use of postwar decentralization of power by forming its own Toyota Automobile Sales Association ahead of the competition. Because much of Toyota's production infrastructure had been destroyed in allied bombing during the war, Kiichiro, in April 1946, created a reconstruction bureau inside the company, and personally led the effort to restore plant facilities and equipment. By 1947, he was back in control of his company and his vision. Toyota rolled out the SA compact passenger car and resumed production of small and large trucks. Toyota sales climbed to 100,000 units in May 1947, giving employees new hope about the company's future. But that optimism would be short-lived. The Dodge Line, a monetary contraction policy drafted by economist Joseph Dodge to, among other objectives, hold down inflation and fix the yen's exchange rate to the dollar, sent the economy on a deflationary spiral. Automobile demand slowed to a trickle, payments were delayed, and Toyota faced a severe liquidity crisis. The Bank of Japan tried to funnel some credit Toyota's way on the condition that it restructure itself, but when salary reductions led management to reduce the payroll by 1,600 workers in April 1950, the Toyota Labor Union went on strike. Taking responsibility for the labor and management strife, Kiichiro in June relinquished his post as president of Toyota Motor Co., and stepped aside to let Toyota Automatic Loom Works president Taiji Ishida come in and handle the situation. "I'm an engineer. I'm not suited to be a manager," confessed Kiichiro, who resigned as company president in 1950. Kiichiro's departure prompted many union members to opt out as well, by accepting voluntary retirement incentives, putting an end to the two-month conflict. Banks resumed the flow of credit Toyota would need to settle its accounts and stave off bankruptcy. At the shareholders general meeting in July 1950, Ishida was officially sworn in as president of Toyota Motor Co., while still retaining his post as president of Toyota Automatic Loom Works. Ishida also brought in a Mitsui Bank regional manager, Fukio Nakagawa, to serve as a senior managing director. Eiji Toyoda, Kiichiro's cousin, took over the manufacturing division.

Then came the Korean War. Truck orders came pouring from the United Nations Command forces in Korea, and the red ink quickly disappeared from Toyota's balance sheets. The company posted huge profits for the year ending March 1951, and was able to provide dividends to shareholders for the first time since the end of World War II. It was an ironic twist of fate that Toyota's survival would once again hinge on the production of trucks for a war effort. Kiichiro's dream of building passenger cars, for a second time, had to be shelved. Upon taking over the presidency at Toyota Motor, Ishida had proclaimed himself as nothing more than a "temporary steward." Once the company's revival had been accomplished, he would turn the reins back over to Kiichiro. Thanks in part to the Korean conflict, Ishida was able to call for Kiichiro's reinstatement as president. While away from Toyota, Kiichiro had kept himself busy working on helicopter and small-engine development, and had seen his blood pressure stabilize. He was nevertheless thrilled by the prospect of returning to Toyota, and fulfilling his dream of building a truly Japanese automobile for the masses. But on March 27, 1952, Kiichiro died of a sudden stroke. He was 57 years old.

The tragic news of Kiichiro's death prompted Ishida to bring Kiichiro's eldest son, Shoichiro, into the company as an executive director. In the meantime, he also focused on priming Eiji Toyoda for eventual leadership. Eiji had been with Toyota Motor since its founding. He had experienced its peaks and troughs, and Ishida was making sure Eiji would earn the valuable experience he needed in both auto production and management.

Eiji Toyoda had been devoting most of his energy to development of the Toyopet Crown, the passenger car project that Kiichiro would certainly have been shepherding had he lived. Eiji was a senior director in 1955 when he saw the Toyopet Crown and Toyopet Master go on sale. In every way, the vehicles were the fulfillment of Kiichiro's dream. The Crown was a tremendous hit and quickly became the country's "passenger car" as envisioned. Eiji was instrumental in leading Toyota on an aggressive modernization and cost-reduction drive through mass production, and soon Toyota owned a 35.2 percent share of the passenger-car market.

Toyopet Crown
Photograph courtesy of Toyota Motor Corp.

Toyota made the first exports of the Crown to the U.S. in 1957. But it didn't fare well. The cars rattled violently on America's highways, and had poor acceleration. Eventually, they were taken off the list of Japanese exports. Still, the experience proved invaluable to Toyota engineers, who came back from America armed with reams of new data on how to make improvements.

Ishida continued a "no borrowing" style of management under his favorite motto of "building one's castle with one's own hands." Ishida is largely credited for having brought Toyota back to profitability, and leading it back to a growth trajectory. He ended up serving as company president for 11 years until 1961, and has favorably come to be regarded in almost "Lincoln-like" terms as the savior of Toyota. While the company's day-to-day management had mostly been handled by Ishida and Eiji, Ishida relinquished the presidency to former Mitsui banker, Fukio Nakagawa, and quietly receded into the background role of Toyota chairman.

Eiji Toyoda was promoted to executive vice president in 1962 and continued to spearhead Toyota's passenger-car development amid the rapid growth and motorization of Japan in the postwar period. In 1966, the Toyota Corolla burst onto the scene as an instant hit, and established Toyota as the undisputed leader of the production automobile. When Nakagawa died of a heart attack the following year in 1967, the time was finally ripe for Eiji Toyoda, now 54, to take over. The biggest challenges he would face during his tenure would arrive with

Toyota Corolla
Photograph courtesy of Toyota Motor Corp.

the oil crises in the 1970s and the advent of regulatory emissions standards. But Eiji still managed to steer his family's company to record breaking profits. Moreover, Eiji would lead Toyota's globalization drive, and when the crush of Japanese imports to American shores led to trade frictions between the U.S. and Japan, Eiji Toyoda would take the initiative in implementing voluntary export controls and forging strategic partnerships with overseas rivals such as GM. The NUMMI plant in California, where GM and Toyota agreed to share automobile-production platforms and technologies, has become a textbook model for joint-venture partnerships, and was the first of its kind in the automotive industry.

Toyota's postwar restructuring drive had also led to the separation of Toyota Motor Sales from Toyota Motor. But Eiji brought them together again in 1982 as the reconsolidated Toyota Motor Corp., of which he became the first chairman. Kiichiro's eldest son, Shoichiro now 57, assumed the office of president.

The Shoichiro Toyoda period saw increased globalization efforts through the establishment of production bases abroad, including construction of a plant in Kentucky. These efforts gave Toyota the financial diversity and strength to grow despite the rapid rise of the yen after the Plaza Agreement in September 1985, which depreciated the dollar against other major Western currencies. As had Eiji, Shoichiro endeavored to break Toyota out of an introspective company culture that had been fostered under Ishida, instead emphasizing bold action and dialogue. Shoichiro became the essential spokesman for "Japan Inc." in 1994, as chairman of the *Keidanren*, the Japan Business Federation. But by the time Shoichiro became chairman and stepped down as company president in 1992 to make way for his younger brother, Tatsuro, Toyota was again facing new challenges as immense as those encountered during the Ishida days.

Domestic demand for automobiles had grown anemic since the bursting of the bubble economy in the early 1990s, compounded by a rapidly appreciating yen against the dollar. Then Tatsuro Toyoda was suddenly hospitalized with high blood pressure. Toyota chairman Shoichiro Toyoda stepped in to ride out the crisis, but eventually appointed a non-family member, Hiroshi Okuda, to lead the company in Tatsuro's place. This bore a striking resemblance to the situation decades earlier when the Toyoda family leader, Kiichiro, elected to abdicate leadership to someone inside the organization, Taizo Ishida, who was capable of leading the company through change. This time, the job would fall to 62-year-old executive vice president Okuda.

"Assuming this office at my age poses mental and physical challenges. But for the Toyota group and Japan, I will do my utmost," said Okuda at the August 1995 press conference to announce his appointment. Like Ishida, Okuda was a keen believer in sound capitalist and business principles over tradition. In an age of intensifying global competition, those would be the drivers of change. "A Toyota unwilling to change poses the biggest threat to our future," Okuda told his managers. "Let's become proponents of trial and error. Let's be willing to take bold risks, and then apply fair and proper assessments to their results."

Hiroshi Okuda
Photograph courtesy of Toyota Motor Corp.

Okuda set out to break the stale atmosphere that had begun to permeate the company, and to foster a spirit of activism. Toyota had been late in entering the booming RV market, so it began churning out a slew of new models, while investing more resources in the globally strategic small-car market. In 1999, the Toyota Vitz, the Yaris outside of Japan, became an instant hit among younger consumers. Okuda also shifted emphasis to an eco-strategy that would ultimately lead to the world's first mass-market hybrid passenger car, the Prius.

As a result, Toyota built its domestic share back up to the 40 percent level, and re-emerged from its efforts stronger than ever. Okuda's straightforward style of talk and action gradually won him the admiration and respect of the business world, and in 1999, he followed his predecessors into the chairmanship of *Keidanren*. But only four years into his presidency at Toyota, Okuda turned the leadership over to 62-year-old Fujio Cho. Cho would be the second Toyoda family outsider to head the company since 1995.

"Okuda-*san* has shown us the road we must take. I plan to bring further clarity to that path," spoke Cho at the announcement of his appointment. Cho vowed to put in place the structures capable of ensuring that the Toyota DNA, which the founders had created and Okuda had reestablished during his tenure, would be passed on to coming generations, regardless of whether or not a Toyoda family member was at the helm. Cho articulated the "Toyota Way," a set of beliefs that could be shared and understood by employees and partners the world over.

Completion of the "Toyota *Koryo*"

Throughout its history, Toyota has been characterized by strong, consistent and talented leadership, and today has grown accustomed to being run by people outside of the Toyoda family bloodline. Although there is every reason to believe that at some point, Akio Toyoda—son of honorary chairman Shoichiro, and grandson of Kiichiro—will one day be president, it is not a foregone conclusion, especially when considering that the Toyoda family shareholding ratio is low. But the Toyoda family continues to command great reverence and respect, and will always be a unifying force for the entire Toyota group, particularly in the codified form of the *koryo* or Toyota Way.

In commemoration of Toyota Motor's seventieth anniversary in 2007, Katsuaki Watanabe had the *koryo* specially printed onto his business cards, pointing to the particular significance of the second mandate: "remaining at the vanguard of the times," as having never been more salient than now. He greatly credits Cho for his effective efforts in re-expressing the *koryo* for today's world.

Cho was born February 2, 1937 in Dalian, part of then Japanese-controlled Manchuria. He was the eldest son of a Manchuria railway worker. His father, Yoshitake, remembers how people would immediately begin speaking to him in Chinese upon learning his name was "Cho." He therefore gave his son a distinctly Japanese first name, Fujio, which translates as "man of Fuji." When the war ended, Cho was a third-grader in Peking (Beijing). He moved with his family back to Tokyo, where he attended high school, and excelled in the martial art of *kendo*. He then gained entry to Tokyo University's law department, the fast track for future leaders, where again he devoted himself to practicing *kendo*. It was at the strong urging of his one of his *kendo* mentors that Cho joined Toyota in 1960.

In his sixth year, Cho was assigned to the production-administration division, where he received instruction in production-system efficiency and waste reduction under the direct tutelage of Taichi Ono and Kikuo Suzumura, two men who were instrumental in advancing the "lean manufacturing" processes created by founding fathers Sakichi and Kiichiro, which aimed at reducing error, eliminating waste, and improving production performance.

Toyota's lean manufacturing continues to serve as a model for manufacturers around the world.

Stopping an entire assembly line, for example, because of a solitary defect resulting from the error of one person would lead to tremendous waste in efficiency. So onsite foremen were empowered with extensive factory-floor authority to boost quality controls. When a problem arose, it would undergo repeated questioning and examination until its roots could be traced, and a *kaizen* or improvement measure be put in place to prevent that same problem from occurring again.

In 1987, Cho was transferred to the U.S. as vice president of Toyota Motor Manufacturing USA, where he was to build a plant in Kentucky. There he was able to share with his American colleagues the manufacturing lessons he'd learned from Ono, which helped Cho earn the trust of his American colleagues and the local community, and turned the Kentucky plant into a major success. In 1994, Cho returned to Japan, and was appointed senior managing director in charge of public relations and external affairs for all of Toyota. It was a position tailormade for him. The U.S. and Japan were involved in heated auto-trade talks, at the time, over opening the Japanese market more to American autos and components. Cho was able to call upon his extensive personal networks and experiences from his time in the U.S. to craft an appropriate response and effective global strategy, with president Hiroshi Okuda and chairman Shoichiro Toyoda, to move Toyota forward in a changing competitive landscape.

Cho's tenure as Toyota president spanned from 1989 to 2005, when he worked assiduously to build Toyota's global footprint while maintaining a better than 40 percent share of a shrinking Japanese car market. Perhaps most importantly, Cho continued the crusade he had begun in Kentucky years earlier to spread the word of the Toyota Way to employees throughout the world, bringing the message of Taichi Ono and Toyota founders to new Toyota members everywhere.

Watanabe succeeded Cho in February 2005. When asked upon his appointment what strengths he would bring to the office, Watanabe replied, "The ability to raise team objectives and tackle them together."

Watanabe immediately joined Toyota upon graduating from the prestigious and privately run Keio University in Tokyo in 1964. He was assigned to various key divisions, including those for procurement and production. During his senior managing director days from 2000, he masterminded the "CCC21" plan aimed at reducing costs by an average of 30 percent across the board. In three years, a trillion yen had been shaved off the cost structure, which Watanabe humbly credited to the use of inherent strengths at Toyota.

"What we essentially accomplished was nothing more than the aggregate of many minor improvements, or *kaizen*. I have always been an advocate of taking an honest and thorough, step-by-step approach to things."

Cho and Watanabe both focus on utilizing and strengthening functional roles inside the company over exhibiting charismatic leadership, to disseminate the Toyota Way. Under Cho, Toyota established the Toyota Institute, a training facility with an emphasis on internal education and activities designed to pass on the Toyota DNA, to succeeding generations. A booklet entitled the *Toyota Way* was compiled in 2001, again, based on the *koryo*.

Toyota's leadership in the clean-car war certainly owes much to the company's concerted effects to carry forward the message of its founders, Sakichi and Kiichiro Toyoda, as a means for inspiring, enlightening, and uniting its people.

Soichiro Honda's Dream

In contrast to Toyota's meticulous, down-to-earth style of management, Honda describes its form of leadership as the "pursuit of dreams."

On November 17, 2006, I was in the Peacock Room of Tokyo's Imperial Hotel to attend the annual Honda Prize ceremony, being presented by the Honda Foundation. The event was taking place on the hundredth anniversary of Soichiro Honda's birth.

"Technology has brought me to where I am today, and if technology can help solve the problems in our world, then that's where I want to enlist my services," Soichiro had said upon establishing the foundation years before. "Whether it's scholarship or technology, everything in this world should be put in the service of mankind. The most important thing is to have a heart full of love and regard for your fellow man."

For someone who had risen from an automotive mechanic to president of a world-class auto company, the words "dream" and "technology" were inextricably linked.

Takeo Fukui opened the event by saying, "It is truly a wonderful and joyous thing that the Honda Prize, which began with the aim of ensuring that technological development benefits mankind, falls today on the birthday of our company founder."

On display at the entrance to the hall was the Honda Cub, the motorbike that first turned Soichiro's boyhood dream into reality, along with the first four-wheeled automobile that Honda manufactured. The same exhibit was also put on proud display on the first floor showroom of the Honda office in Tokyo's Aoyama district.

As at Toyota, the people at Honda harbor a rich tradition of sharing ideas and knowledge, and a healthy sense of crisis. They engage in free and exuberant discussions, arrive at new conclusions, and dive into their work with unqualified enthusiasm. For a while, there was a movement to change this "*waigaya*" style in reaction to the asset bubble's collapse in the 1990s. Honda "reacted" more than it "acted." But Fukui, in calling for a return to Honda's "riverhead principles," seeks to recapture the free-thinking, creative spirit of its engineers and its starry-eyed founder. Honda had once sat astride the world in clean-car technology. It owed its automotive existence to it. This is the kind of history that warranted repeating.

Wireless Generator Engine for Bicycles?

Soichiro Honda was born on November 17, 1906, in a village called Komyomura near Hamamatsu in Shizuoka prefecture. His father was a honest, hard-working blacksmith, with great tinkering skills, and his mother an expert seamstress. They were poor, but Honda was able to live a free and uninhibited childhood. Inheriting his parents' dexterity, he nurtured a strong curiosity in machines. He was so moved the first time he saw an automobile in town, he felt his heart flutter with excitement at the smell of gasoline and the blue smoke the vehicle belched as it chugged on by. "I stuck my nose right up to the oil slick the car had deposited on the road, and breathed in its wonderful odor," Honda fondly recalled. After graduating from grade school in 1922, Honda at 15 became an apprentice at an auto-repair shop in Tokyo called Art Shokai, where he is said to have reveled in his release from the country ethic of drab thriftiness, arriving at work each day in loud shirts and ties. There he saw a wide variety of cars being brought in for repairs, from Mercedes to Lincolns. Needless to say, Honda had a ravenous appetite for knowledge, and

Soichiro Honda
Photograph courtesy of Honda Motor Co.

this kind of shop-floor work was like a taste of heaven. The real-life experience he acquired in fixing cars and parts would serve him well throughout his life.

Honda proved so adept at his work that he was allowed to open up an Art Shokai branch in his hometown of Hamamatsu in 1928. But his dissatisfaction with the apprenticeship-based repair business and a growing interest in piston rings prompted him to establish his own company, Tokai Precision Machinery, which would eventually be destroyed by U.S. bombers in World War II.

It wasn't until some time after the war that Soichiro was given an old army wireless generator engine, and struck upon the idea of attaching it to a bicycle as a supplementary power source. In a barracks he built on a war-scorched field in Hamamatsu, Honda raised the *Honda Giken* sign, and proceeded to buy up the remaining No. 5 wireless generator engines, approximately 500 of them, which he rebuilt with a power component, and sold as a motor for bicycles.

This customized engine fared well enough on the market for Honda to next try his hand at building an original engine from scratch, resulting in the first Honda original product, the Honda

Model A bicycle engine. In November, 1947, he began producing and selling motor-attached bicycles. They were an instant hit in a postwar period when bicycles were still a rarity. The next banner Honda raised was that of "*Honda Giken Kogyo*" (literally "Honda Technical Research Industrial"), or the "Honda Motor Co." It started as a tiny, one-room office, but became Soichiro's fortress of invention. Honda founded the Honda Motor Co. with capital of one million yen on September 24, 1948. He was already 41 years old.

In August 1949, he developed and began selling the Dream D, a much more powerful Model A, with a design that would put it in the category of a "motorcycle," and his venture into two-wheeled vehicle production began in earnest. Soon afterwards, a friend introduced him to a man named Takeo Fujisawa. The two hit it off immediately. Fujisawa joined Honda as managing director, and a long partnership began, with one man as the "builder" and the other as the "seller."

The Principle of "Three Joys"

In September 1950, Honda moved his base of operations away from Hamamatsu to Tokyo. After hiring his first school-trained engineer in Kiyoshi Kawashima, he set aside a corner of the factory so the two could get to work on installing the first four-stroke engine in a Dream E motorcycle. Although it was a small 150-cc two-wheeled vehicle, it was capable of generating considerably more power than the same class of vehicles from other makers, and easily handled the mountainous curves of the Hakone Pass. It marked the beginning of the four-stroke Honda. Within six months after production began, Honda was selling 500 units a month. A year later, the number rose to 2,000 units, and in three years time, 2,600, vaulting Honda into the national spotlight.

Based on these experiences, Honda laid out in the *Honda Monthly Report* his "Three Joys," which would form the basis of the Honda philosophy. They were: "the joy of producing, the joy of selling, and the joy of buying." Honda elaborated:

The first of these, the joy of producing, is a joy known only to the engineer. Just as the Creator used an abundant will to create in making all the things that exist in the natural universe, so the engineer uses his own ideas to create products and contribute to society. This is a happiness that can hardly be compared to anything else. Furthermore, when that product is of superior quality so that society welcomes it, the engineers joy is absolutely not to be surpassed. As an engineer myself, I am constantly working in the hope of making this kind of product.

The second joy belongs to the person who sells the product. Our company is a manufacturer. The products made by our company pass into the possession of the various people who have a demand for them through the cooperation and efforts of all our agents and dealers. In this situation, when the product is of high quality, its performance is superior, and its price is reasonable, then it goes without saying that the people who engage in selling it will experience joy. Good, inexpensive items will always find a welcome. What sells well generates profits, as well as pride and happiness in handling those items. A manufacturer of products that do not bring this joy to people who sell those products is disqualified from being a manufacturer worthy of the name.

The third, the joy of the person who buys the product, is the fairest determiner of the products value. It is neither the manufacturer nor the dealer that best knows the value of the product and passes final judgment on it. Rather, it is none other than the purchaser who uses the product in his daily life. There is happiness in thinking, "Oh, I'm so glad I bought this." This joy is the garland that is placed upon the products value. I am quietly confident that the value of our company's products is well advertised by those products themselves. This is because I believe that they give joy to the people who buy them.

The Three Joys form our company's motto. I am devoting all my strength in order to bring them to reality.

(From Honda, Soichiro 1951, "The Three Joys",
Honda Monthly, *no. 4, December 1)*

In March 1952, Soichiro's company completed its latest motor-assisted bicycle, the Model F prototype. Going with die casting as much as possible, the white tank against a red engine design in a lightweight two-stroke, 50-cc engine was by anyone's standards a very smart-looking piece of machinery, the Cub F. And as if he had been waiting for this moment all his life, Fujisawa stepped in to lead the mass-marketing offensive after being with the company only a few months. He sent mail to some 50,000 bicycle shops around the country, and began building a sales network, where previous sales had been through consignment with bicycle retailers. He bought a company propeller airplane to strafe the countryside with advertisement fliers, and sold the Cub F through ingenious methods such as letting a dancing team drive them in a parade. It was a dynamic ad campaign, which proved very effective, and the Cub recorded robust sales, enabling Honda to establish its own sales channels. It was an experience that Honda would find very useful in pioneering a new market for its products—the U.S.

Honda's Creed and Management Policy

"You can't expect to walk ahead of the pack unless you're willing to light the way. If your path is lit by someone else, then you may not be stumbling along, but you are still simply following." Those were words that Fujisawa eventually wrote in his *Hold the Torch Yourself* (The Sanno Institute of Management publications), in which he shared his experiences of building the Honda marketing network.

Honda also laid out his Company Principle in January 1956.

> Maintaining an international viewpoint, we are dedicated to supplying products of the highest efficiency, yet at reasonable prices, for worldwide customer satisfaction.
>
> In making our company grow, we do not expect only to bring well-being to ourselves as employees and to our stockholders.
>
> We seek to provide good products to make our customers happy and to help our affiliated companies prosper. Furthermore, we seek to raise the technological level of Japanese industry and to make a greater contribution to society. These are the purposes for our company's existence.

This was followed by the company's operating policy.

- "Proceed always with ambition and youthfulness."

> We must keep pace with the technological advancements of our world, and lead Japanese industry. So that we can overcome the many obstacles and difficulties that may lie in the road, we need great strength to hold ourselves to great ideals and remain youthful.

- "Respect sound theory, develop fresh ideas and make the most effective use of time."

The best products stand above the highest doctrine. Advanced ideas enable the exponential development of theory. Seek to advance theories, respect ideas and you will find the basis of our development.

- "Enjoy your work, and always brighten your work atmosphere."

There's nothing more joyful than having a good workplace where one can truly and passionately apply oneself. We always pay the deepest respect to others' perspectives, and value the importance of recognizing each other's unique virtues. The work place is where we can polish our personalities; a place where we can become complete individuals. Building a work environment where we can each truly devote our lives is the path to the pursuit of happiness as a whole, and for that purpose we must all strive together.

- "Strive constantly for a harmonious flow of work."

In order to produce superior products, like an orchestra producing wonderful music, people, machines and various equipment and facilities, many functions must beat with one rhythm, and must flow like a stream. In the large company rhythm, each individual employee, from production to sales, should feel like an indispensable part of a greater whole.

- "Be ever mindful of the value of research and endeavor."

We live in an age of high global competition, and to build a solid bedrock for our company requires unflagging research and effort. Always prepare for the future, never be satisfied with the present. It is imperative that we actively seek to improve ourselves daily. If we can abide by these principles, we can simultaneously succeed in achieving the joy of the builder, the joy of the seller and the joy of the buyer.

The original source of Honda's current creed and corporate management principles come from essays written by Soichiro Honda in the company newsletter, but the concepts of "limitless dreams and youthfulness" have been carried forward as a spiritual foundation for the company.

Building a Spirit of Free Culture and Dreams into Environmental Effort

Japan considered 1955 its greatest year of prosperity, and called it *"jimmukei-ki"* in reference to Japan's first emperor, Jimmu. It was the year that saw the first Toyota Toyopet Crown, and the sale of the first transistor radio by a little known company called *"Tokyo Tsushin Kogyo"* (Sony). In this year, Honda unveiled the 350-cc, Dream SB, the 250-cc Dream SA, and a new top-of-the-line motorcycle housing Honda's first OHC, overhead camshaft engine, with more than 10 horsepower. In 1957, Honda released a 250-cc, two-stroke, two-cylinder motorcycle, which was suitable for export, the first high-revolution, high-output engine Dream C70.

Even after this prosperous period ended, Honda continued to soar, becoming the nation's number one volume producer of two-wheeled vehicles. Then in August 1958, Honda installed a high-revolution, high-output 50-cc, four-stroke engine in the Super Cub. Beautiful to look at, it was viewed as an auto bike for women as well as men, and for the rest of the century, was produced relatively unaltered. The Super Cub has been deemed a masterpiece of engineering. In October 1962, building on its achievements in motorcycles, Honda exhibited its first ever four-wheeled vehicles at the ninth All Japan Motor, paving the way for its debut as an automobile company of the future.

58 Super Cub
Photograph courtesy of Honda Motor Co.

In terms of Honda management, the early Honda spirit of dreams and youthfulness that Soichiro Honda had touted became its source of continued strength. Honda's current green strategy lies squarely within those core beliefs. A research climate and culture that encourages engineers to give free play to their imaginations has always been central to the Honda philosophy, and would eventually lead to the establishment of Honda R&D in 1960 as a fully independent entity with its own headquarters and production.

"We must embark upon a new form of personnel management for the Research Center; one that combines the abilities of individual researchers as equal partners and enhances their collective wisdom," said Takeo Fujisawa, in response to a question about the spinoff. He noted that independence was given to the research arm with the intention of cultivating experts of peerless skills in their respective fields, and then giving them an environment conducive to research; a system and a place where they could give birth to wonderfully new, world-class ideas.

Soichiro Honda served as Honda R&D's first president, establishing a precedent for future leaders of Honda, who would preside over the research facility before assuming the overall company reins. Honda presidents from Nobuhiko Kawamoto to Shigeyuki Yoshino, and now Takeo Fukui, have all had the experience of serving as Honda R&D presidents. "We cannot succeed in this highly competitive world unless we spend a great amount of time on creativity," said Honda at the company's inauguration. "Japan is a country that has traditionally prospered on the strength of its ideas."

It is a philosophy written into the company prospectus as well. "We must first create an environment in which researchers can concentrate on key issues relating to their expertise, without having to worry about time, job ranking, or other formalities."

Honda, in re-examining its roots for clues to the future, knows that the key to its success in the clean-car war lies in taking its own path. Toyota, which has historically been more of a well-executing follower than an independent trailblazer, has with the success of its hybrid technology almost taken a page from Honda's book. If so, then Honda can find encouragement from what would appear an affirmation of its core beliefs; that with a climate of freedom in the pursuit of dreams, it has what it takes to win the clean-car war.

Conclusion

In early 2007, when attention began to focus on whether Toyota would surpass GM in global volume of auto sales, GM was stepping up its presence and demonstrating its strength in China and other emerging auto markets. As the calendar year drew to a close, Toyota and GM were running pretty even, with GM slightly ahead. Even so, Toyota looks to be on the offensive. As I was writing this, the United Auto Workers union in the U.S. had gone on strike, and was working to hammer out an agreement with GM over the handling of healthcare benefits for retirees.

But despite their current positions, both Toyota and GM find themselves at the start of a new century facing a landscape not unlike that which GM and Ford faced early in the past century. With the era of the gasoline combustion engine drawing to a close, the field is once again wide open to anyone who can come up with the best new alternative. In that sense, every auto company is starting from scratch.

Japan's "Big Three" automakers of Toyota, Nissan, and Honda used the 2007 Tokyo Motor Show to demonstrate and declare their commitments to an automotive future that is both prosperous and environmentally friendly. Although they claim to have taken the lead in shaping the automotive future, the truth is that all the world's major auto companies are spending billions of dollars on R&D as a matter of necessity. Even the BRIC countries of Brazil, Russia, India, and China, which will play a leading role in the growth of the auto sector in the twenty-first century, are consciously looking for ways to secure the growth of their economies within a more ecologically sustainable context.

As the world's largest market, the U.S. will continue to be the main battleground in the "clean-car war" in the medium term. And emotions could run high if one or two of the major domestic players fail to survive the shakeout. But in the end, it will be technology, and consumer acceptance of that technology, that serve as final arbiters in the fight, whether it is EVs, hydrogen fuel cells, biomass, or something completely different. In all likelihood, the leading technologies will vary depending upon a particular country or region's particular needs, traits, and resources. But the shift to renewable energy sources looks certain.

Toyota and Honda have emerged strongest in the early days of this transitional period, and have received market validation, which is helping them gain the confidence and the financial base they will need to move aggressively forward. For that reason, I see them as having a distinct edge over the competition, because it builds the resources they need to keep pace with developments in all other emerging technologies, from the advances that European companies are making in diesel, to the flex-fuel and plug-in EV programs that U.S. rivals are pursuing. Battery and fuel-cell technologies, for example, are key areas in which all auto market players, with any hope of surviving, will want to exhibit cutting-edge leadership. The partnerships and cross-industry alliances I have described earlier could shape future fortunes to a great degree.

Finally, there is the end-user. Toyota managed to get a headstart in the twenty-first century because it acted quickly to manifest its vision of the future. But that effort would have ended in vain had not the consumer cast its vote in its favor. Not many in the auto industry expected hybrids to sell, or that they would amount to much more than a bridge to the coming new automotive paradigm. But consumers proved that they, too, had a vision of the future, be it positive or negative, and felt compelled to act on it. I therefore hope readers of this book will come away with a keener sense of what possibilities lie ahead for them as key stakeholders in an increasingly automotive and, hopefully, sustainable world.

Bibliography

Diesel, Rudolf Christian Karl. *How the Diesel Engine Came to Be*, translated by Shigeki Yamaoka, Tokyo: Sankaido Publishing Co., 1993.

Fujimoto, Takahiro. *The Japanese 'Mono-zukuri' Way*, Tokyo: Nikkei Inc., 2004.

Gore, Al. *An Inconvenient Truth*, translated by Junko Edahiro, Tokyo: Random House Kodansha Co., Ltd., 2007.

Hasegawa, Yozo, *Would You Like to Work for Carlos Ghosn?*, Tokyo: Nikkei Business Publications, Nikkei Inc., 2001

Hasegawa, Yozo. *Lexus: The Toyota Challenge*, Tokyo: Nikkei Inc., 2005

Honda Motor Co. *A Story for Posterity—The 50-year Challenge*, Tokyo: Honda Motor Co., 1999.

Iemura, Hiroaki. *The Prius Dream*, Tokyo: Futabasha Publishers Ltd., 1999.

Iizuka, Shozo. *The Potential of Fuel Cell and Electric Vehicles*, Tokyo: Grand Prix Publishing Co., 2006.

Ikari, Yoshiakira. *Age of the Hybrid Car*, Tokyo: Kojinsha, 1999.

Ikehara, Teruo. *Toyota vs. Honda*, Tokyo: The Nikkan Kogyo Shimbun, Ltd., 2002.

Japan Institute of Invention and Innovation, *70 Year History of the Japan Institute of Invention and Innovation.*, 1974.

Kajiwara, Meisetsu. *Cleaning Up Diesel Emissions*, Tokyo: CMC Publishing Co, 2006.

Liker, Jeffrey K. *The Toyota Way*, translated by Kimio Inagaki, Tokyo: Nikkei Business Publications, Inc., 2004.

Mihori, Naotsugu. *The New Prius Future Car—Engineers' Challenge*, Tokyo: Nikkei Business Publications, Inc., 2004.

Nikkei Business Daily & Nikkei Inc. *The Honda Reformation.* Tokyo: Nikkei Inc., 2005.

Nikkei Business Publications. *Complete Guide to Hybrid and Electric Cars 2007*, Nikkei Business Publications, Tokyo: Nikkei Inc., 2006.

Nikkei Inc. *The Okuda-ism that Transformed Toyota*, Tokyo: Nikkei Inc., Nikkei Business Bunko., 2004.

Noguchi, Hitoshi, *Kiichiro Toyoda: The Man Who Built Toyota*, Tokyo: WAC Publishing Co., 2002.

Seiff, Ingo. *Mercedes Benz: Portrait of a Legend*, translated by Akihiko Nakamura, Tokyo: Kodansha Ltd., 1999.

Sloan, Jr., Alfred P. *My Years With General Motors*, translated by Yuko Ariga, Tokyo: Diamond, Inc., 2003.

Sugimoto, Kazutoshi. *The Diesel Car Explained*, Tokyo: Sankaido Publishing Co., 2006.

Toyota Group. *Kizuna,*. Toyota Group, 2005

Toyota Motor Co. *In Toyota's Steps*, Toyota Motor Co., 1978.

Toyota Motor Corp. *Limitless Production: 50 Years of Toyota Cars*, Toyota Motor Corp., 1987.

Tsukamoto, Kiyoshi. *Why Hollywood Stars Drive Hybrid Cars*, Tokyo: Asahi Shimbun Co., 2006.

Wada, Kazuo & Yui, Tsunehiko. *Kiichi Toyoda: A Biography*, Nagoya: The University of Nagoya Press, 2002.

Zemma, Takanori. *Toyota vs. Benz vs. Honda*, Tokyo: Kodansha Ltd., 2002.

Index